READY, SET, LAUNCH

FOREWARD BY RICHARD DOLAN

READY, SET, LAUNCH

THE ESSENTIAL PLAYBOOK FOR ENTREPRENEURS

BY COURTNEY JARED BANNAN, ESQ.

First Edition 2024
ISBN: 979-8-9902798-0-3 Paperback
979-8-9902798-1-0 Hardcover
Library of Congress Control Number: 2024905743

This book is intended for informational purposes only and should not be construed as legal advice. The information provided within these pages is not a substitute for professional legal counsel. The author and publisher make no representations or warranties regarding the accuracy or completeness of the information presented herein.

Readers are advised to consult with a qualified legal professional for advice specific to their individual circumstances. The content of this book is general in nature and may not be applicable to all situations. Laws and regulations vary and are subject to change, and the information contained in this book may not be up to date.

The author and publisher disclaim any liability for any actions taken or not taken based on the information provided in this book. There is no guarantee of specific outcomes or results as a result of using the information contained herein.

Readers are encouraged to verify the information provided and seek legal advice from qualified professionals before making decisions or taking actions that may have legal consequences.

Socrates Publishing
Fort Lauderdale, Florida

Typeset by Michelle Cline

PREFACE

This book was a beautiful journey to write.

My entrepreneurial pursuits began when I was a stay-at-home mom to my firstborn son, writing articles for local newspapers. He was such a good baby that I grew bored and decided to apply to law school while he was napping.

I got accepted to law school and found out I was pregnant with my second baby a week before my full-time semester started. I went straight through as a full-time student, gave birth to a perfect little girl in the middle of second semester, became an editor of the *International Law Journal,* worked as a co-author on a citation book, and authored papers on Caribbean law and international commerce and trade.

I sold real estate on weekends and evenings to pay for it all. Yes, I am a classic hardworking overachiever.

Eight years later, I was asked to teach a class called "Law Office Management" as an adjunct professor at my alma mater.

This book began as a supplement for that class, which was essentially turning law students into Lawyerpreneurs. There was not a great deal of material on this subject, so I started creating my own, and this was officially titled "Professor Bannan's Class Supplement" in its preliminary stages.

As digital marketing became more popular and lawyers were regulated by the state bar in addition to the federal regulations, I saw an increasing need to teach students about social media marketing pitfalls.

Additionally, my clients all had great business concepts but no idea that internet promotions are shark-infested waters for regulatory concerns. Or why a C Corp may be better than an S Corp.

Then, I became a tech entrepreneur and saw another, deeper need for content that helped entrepreneurs comprehend simple business structures, business concepts, and the avoidance of legal issues.

And above all else, I wanted to do something with purpose and intent – to be mindful and embrace my spirituality by helping others.

Lastly, after working in the influencer space for so long, I saw how all of this tied together with mindset and the unique personality traits shared by all entrepreneurs.

And that is the story behind this playbook.
This is dedicated to everyone who helped me become who I am – whether through love, support or lessons learned. Lessons and Blessings were abundant.

**Visit www.courtneyjaredbannan.com
https://www.instagram.com/courtneyjaredbannanesquire/**

FOREWORD

Dear Reader,

I have had the profound privilege of working with many of history's most iconic legends and Gods of commerce and culture over the past three decades. And almost always they have someone that serves a role performed by someone like Courtney Jared Bannan.

But in truth, no one is quite like Courtney.

You see, unlike those I've met that advise, lead, and navigate clients through thick or thin, Courtney demonstrates and embodies an incredibly unique gift, talent and set of skills.

In addition to being an attorney and counselor in multiple areas of law ranging from real estate to securities, commercial and entertainment law; Courtney most importantly understands business.

This is why Courtney is the most sought after lawyer of the land— not just because she is brilliant within that realm; but she also understands the psychology and playing field for entrepreneurs like you and me.

I encourage you to not simply read this book but follow its wisdom for I am certain it was forged in the fires of experience, expertise and empathy afforded by the years of professional prowess and practice of Courtney.

This book, *"Ready, Set, Launch: The Essential Playbook for Entrepreneurs"* is a heartfelt companion for entrepreneurs embarking on a new venture where Courtney leads the way for you and your thoughts on business with passion, power, and precision. But I warn you, this book will irreversibly transform your relationship to what's next.

I appreciate the efforts and energy Courtney poured into these pages as her investment manifested in kind through her very own ups and downs; shared through her stories celebrating creativity, innovation and the power of purpose and mindset.

This is the first book I've read in a long time that elevates and emboldens the entrepreneurial spirit and need for vision. This is likely because Courtney is an instrument for impact, having practiced for purpose—and not just profit.

She is my friend, and now your Sherpa for success. But I promise you, you'll discover this is not just a lady of law; but more critically a lady of leadership, life, and legacy.

Enjoy this educational journey and be sure to love every minute of it.

Richard Dolan
www.richarddolan.com
https://www.instagram.com/richard.dolan/
https://www.instagram.com/the.richworld/

TABLE OF CONTENTS

CHAPTER 1:

THE ENTREPRENEURIAL MINDSET

Look in the mirror. Who do you see? Are you a visionary with an entrepreneurial idea? Are you a creative person who sees a market gap as an opportunity to invent new products or services? Are you a record-breaking salesperson with a huge skill set that can sell any product? Are you a risk taker, a multitasking organizer, and an opportunist? Are you a business coach with a targeted audience? Are you an attorney with a niche market looking to open a boutique firm? Are you a personal trainer with a unique vision? Are you a chiropractor looking to open a health and wellness center?

Write down who you are and what you bring to the table.

Then ask someone else to do it for you and see how they perceive you.

Knowing who you are and what drives you is the most key factor in your success. It is your "why." It is your fire, your fuel, and your sustainable energy. It is your brand.

The fact that you are reading this book means you are ready to be an entrepreneur. Now we just need to dive a little deeper to create a pathway to success.

What are the distinct traits of entrepreneurs? Entrepreneurs are imaginative and provoked by life around them. Entrepreneurs see problems as opportunities to create solutions. They are dreamers, builders, and forward thinkers. They are strategic, motivational, and highly driven by personal motives. They are, in essence, the creative energy of the universe helping us move forward into the future on a wave of innovation.

Nine-to-five workers have a different skill set and may have more of an operational acumen, but they are driven by security and are more influenced by a steady paycheck than innovation. We need them—they organize things! They process things! Most importantly, they buy things! They work all day and need the services and products entrepreneurs create. They like the security and balance of their world, and we like excitement and unpredictability.

A nine-to-fiver has more of a *"don't fix if it ain't broke"* mindset, whereas the entrepreneur, after a period of time, will want to smash and shatter one solid idea in order to use the pieces to create many different ideas. We are disrupters and rabble-rousers. We are always looking for an outlet for that overwhelming passion to create and build something to destroy normalcy and invoke great awe. We fear being basic, boring, and bored.

You are reading this because you have an idea. A vision. A product. An invention. A service. A company that you want to grow. A desire to be MORE. A desire to do MORE. You may be a young person with a novel idea and no money; you may be a serial entrepreneur that has tried dozens of different ventures; or you may be a well-off person that is employed full-time somewhere, and you are looking for freedom from boredom.

You may be a professional in a field, such as law, and you want to open your own boutique or specialized law firm. You may be a realtor looking to build a brand and find a unique way to approach home buying; you may have a niche market that you want to dominate.

This book applies to all of you visionaries looking to work for yourself, whether it is full-time, part-time, or your side hustle.

Do you have what it takes to be an entrepreneur? YES! Everyone does. For some people, it may be very natural, and for others, it may take some work. Think about all the inherent qualities you have—the ones you are born with—that set you apart from other people you know. Also, think about the qualities you have gained from experience and work.

Read the descriptive words below and check all that apply to you. Would you consider yourself:

Passionate		Courageous		Knowledgeable		Street Smart	
Focused		Tenacious		Educated		Ambitious	
Determined		Resilient		Inexhaustible		Fearless	
Analytical		Confident		Flexible		Motivated	
Creative		Innovative		Disruptive		Adaptable	
Solution Oriented		Inventive		Offbeat		Self-Taught	
Forward Thinking		Skilled		A Renegade		Bulletproof	
A Visionary		Experienced		A Catalyst		Book Smart	

Count the number of traits you checked off in the chart. Now, ask someone close to you to check the qualities they think you have. To succeed, you need to be tenacious and confident. You need to be focused and unrelenting. You need to be flexible and resilient.

You need to handle rejection and criticism in order to grow. You also need to be honest with yourself. Like, brutally. Let's get raw.

Most likely, the traits you chose for yourself are who you WANT to be. Your weaknesses are exposed here. The traits your friend chose are how you project yourself to others. If you have any doubt, ask several people to select the traits from that list that embody who you are.

Make a list of the words you did not choose. Evaluate why you do not think those words applied to you. Then evaluate whether you think that is a good thing or a dreadful thing. Take notes of what bothers you; dive into what words you did not select because you felt you were not good enough or smart enough to be those things.

That right there is the part of your mind you need to reset. Why? Because even the qualities you may feel are negative about yourself could be the very ones counterbalancing what makes you...YOU. Those traits are what make you unique. It is your driving force.

Self-reflection and self-awareness are important because, as an entrepreneur, you must do various tasks that require a multitude of talents. You will be talking to people and selling your product; you will be adjusting and bouncing back from rejection; you may be the one starting all over again and moving on to the next idea.

Without the right mindset, this book is useless. The things you will learn will be useless. Your brain, your attitude, and how you process and metabolize information will determine your success. Maybe you do not have as many of those qualities as you thought you did, but hey, that is more than okay! You just may need a "Mindset Reset."

You ARE the machine that makes it all happen, so you need to get your head in the game and stay healthy and focused to get over the finish line too. Do not focus on your weaknesses, just KNOW them, and confront them. Always focus on your strengths and let others do the tasks and activities that are not your strongest suit, then they become another strength. Knowing your weaknesses and how to work around them is a strong point in your personality. If you dislike cold calling and are terrible at it, but you make amazing promotional videos, why on earth would you focus on cold calling? You should focus on those videos and hire someone to do your cold calling or send the videos in lieu of those cold calls.

To really make use of this book, grab a fresh notebook or journal to do the exercises and take notes. Let's do this!

THE MINDSET RESET

If you feel that you fall short of the entrepreneurial mindset but really want to be one, all you need is a reset. The person that you WANT to be IS your future self. You can be anyone you want to be, but getting to be that person requires a little work. Think of it as just a string of tasks and exercises that you must accomplish to achieve the goal of being the best version of yourself and becoming the person you know you can be.

We can get off course in life when we have issues and circumstances that drain our energy. We think we are doing fine because we are handling these issues, but we don't realize that in handling all this extraneous negativity, we are losing the parts of us that make us shine and feed our creativity. It is a little more than burnout; it is also losing momentum in our growth as people and as creative entrepreneurs.

The exercise below is how I reset my mindset when I find myself off course. What words above inspire you? What words above are the traits you aspire to? What words did you select to describe yourself?

Step 1: Take stock of your mental energy level, your physical energy level, your negativity level, and your positivity level. Make a list of all the pending issues that are weighing on your mind, circumstances that are worrying you, and the time-consuming activities (even the fun ones). Then, on a scale of 1–10, with 1 being low energy and 10 being high energy, rate how each issue affects those levels.

Then, think about why you feel that way. For example, maybe you have been working too hard on one sale, so you have missed too many workouts, causing your physical energy to be low. Or you have had to handle a family drama and your mental energy is tapped and you need to self-isolate on weekends. Also, when things happen to us, it can bring a negative energy, but that does not necessarily mean that your positive energy will ebb as the negative energy flows.

Negativity and positivity are not dependent on each other because sometimes when we feel negative, we still have hope to improve our situation, which is the positive energy that we need to harness when we need to reset and recharge.

Sometimes there are time-consuming activities and obligations that provide you with a lot of positive energy but drain you of time and throw you off focus from your work and projects. Nights out with friends, wine, romance, and family obligations all take time. Without adhering to a schedule, you will find yourself stressed out and drained from GOOD things.

You do not need "complete" balance right now, you need focus. Complete balance is for people who want to walk on a treadmill for the rest of their lives.

Bust out of that mindset right now. Balance is overrated for people with an entrepreneurial mindset. I am not suggesting that you ignore your friends and family, but I am saying stay focused and do not do anything you feel will cause you to be thrown off your cycle. Stay the course; you got this.

Take your list of issues and activities and use the below to dissect each one to see where your energy is being drained or replenished. Write it all down with your own hands, get granular, and connect with yourself.

Issue, Problem, Time-Consuming Activities		
This affects my:	Rate from 1-10 (1 is low and 10 is high)	Why?
Physical Energy		
Mental Energy		
Negative Energy		
Positive Energy		

Step 2: Make a grid and write down the descriptive words you chose as your inspiration. Then one activity a day that you **completed** in furtherance of evolving into that habit or trait. Use the example below as a reference. If you did not complete an activity, write that in there too. You are accountable to yourself, and this is your reality. Write it down and connect it to your truth.

Knowledgeable	Read two books this week about business
Educated	Got a certificate of training in marketing
Inexhaustible	Working out every day and sleeping six hours for energy maintenance
Flexible	Did not say no to a new meeting, tried somZething new
Disruptive	Changed my marketing plan to something controversial
Offbeat	Went to a live art installation
A Renegade	Quit my day job to pursue my business full-time

Every single day, without exception, write down at least three things you plan to do daily in order to gain the habits and mindset that you need. Remind yourself to always have a great attitude and to not lose focus in your business endeavors.

Learn how to say no to the activities and people that pull you back from the dream you have of making this business work. Say no to EVERYTHING that does not accelerate your progress and purpose.

If you are working alone, you need to determine your work style and consider your strengths and weaknesses. You need to create a workflow that is achievable and maintainable because you only have yourself to account for—that can be dangerous.

If you are working with a team, great! But you also must keep in mind that you must oversee their motivation as well. There are a lot of models and books on work styles, and that is all wrapped up in psychology.

I have my own lingo and ideas for that, but the concepts are nothing new. You will have a dominant trait, and you will be one or all of these types of people. Rate them in the order of your greatest strength to your weakest strength. If you feel you do not have that trait at all, that is your weakest strength. I showed you mine, now show me yours.

WHAT IS YOUR WORK STYLE?

Work Style	Me	You
The Creator: Great at producing ideas and creative pivots for existing ideas.	3	
The Worker Bee: You can execute the idea; you are good at getting every task done from moving the boxes from the truck to the warehouse, responding to requests, opening the mail, and helping others.	2	
The Talker: You are the one who goes to all the networking groups, makes people and business connections, and gets people interested in the company.	6	
The Salesperson: Cold calls, emails, and demonstrations are your strong point. You are not shy about asking for a sale.	5	
The Marketer: You know exactly how to grab people's attention, and you know exactly what needs to be said to make the business or product get noticed. You know how to use social media to your advantage.	4	
The Business Manager: You see the big picture of everything operationally and how it all works together. You are the thinker and are more cautious about how the idea is executed and what direction to go.	1	

As you can see, there are so many different work styles. Some people have the idea and other people are great at the execution of someone else's idea. Some people are self-starters, while others have the worker bee factory mindset. Some people must have a process in place and make spreadsheets and checklists.

For some, that works, and it gives them a path to follow. For others, they are creating a reason to NOT work, and they get lost in planning the work instead of doing the work. Others roll up their sleeves and get to work, but do not track revenue, don't have a plan, and may make a lot of money right away, but then lose it because they aren't tracking profit and loss or lack the structure to keep it going.

As an entrepreneur, you will be one or all of these styles at one point, but your brilliant and disruptive mindset will know when to pivot and what role to play. You understand the need to be a combination of those mindsets and to make a fluid plan from which you can launch and ignite your idea into a profitable business. If you cannot achieve that with a Mindset Reset, determine your true work style deficits, and surround yourself with a team that fills in those spaces for you.

You will learn so much from reading this book. Not only will this book act like a step-by-step guide to creating, building, and growing your business, but it will also teach you about compliance from a wide range of alphabet soup agencies; some you may never have even heard of before. The FTC. The FCC. The SEC. The EEOC.

You have a lot of inspirational people to pump you up and get you excited about becoming an entrepreneur. Now you need someone to tell you HOW to do it. There is so much out there that can take your great idea and turn it into a legal issue, lawsuit, or even a prison sentence! Not to scare you, but you do not know what you do not know, and I am going to fix that for you right now, so let's get you started NOW.

CHAPTER 2:

GOAL SETTING, MINDFULNESS, AND SELF-AWARENESS

I am a classic overachiever. If it comes with a license or certificate, I want it. I started doing yoga to be fit, and that wasn't enough. I had to become a certified yoga instructor. To me, if I was going to invest all that time doing something, I needed to become a master at it. But what happened was I ended up with a completely changed perspective on life, money, success, and self-awareness. However, although I am still an overachiever, I did learn to embrace the unique qualities in my personality that drive me. The first being self-esteem and self-worth. If I do more, I am worth more, right?

WRONG. What a valuable lesson. I have learned where to target my efforts and how to temper my natural urge to do more.

I do this by writing down my goals. Some of the goals I write down are superfluous and others are achievable. This is how I learn about myself.

After writing down your goals for a lengthy period of time, you begin to uncover the multifaceted and beautiful layers of your aspirations. What truly matters to you? What drives you to succeed? Writing down your goals encourages a deeper exploration of your inner self, leading to a more profound understanding of your personal and professional motivations. In short, you cannot help but grow.

Another topic that is a passion of mine is mindfulness and staying present in the moment. Recently someone told me that they perceive me as someone who has a very adventurous life. I could not stop laughing because my time is predominantly spent writing, reading and being alone in nature.

What they really saw was my ability to make the most from being mindful and present. To me, a bird flying in the sky in front of the rising sun is a major event. I take photographs, write poetry, and make reels from it. Most people don't notice the damn bird or the sunrise. I relish the journey—always.

I find wonder and awe in simple things, and I pay attention to everything. In business, this makes me dangerous. In life, this makes me sweet.

But in the tumultuous life of an entrepreneur, it's easy to get caught up in the frenzy of creating and building. However, true success lies not just in achieving goals but in relishing the journey. Mindfulness—the practice of being fully present in the moment—plays a pivotal role in business by fostering creativity, resilience, and a more profound connection to your objectives.

Writing down your goals is also a mindful act. It requires you to be present, intentional, and focused on yourself in that moment. It is more intimate than most people realize.

The synergy between writing down goals, personal accountability, self-awareness, and mindfulness creates a powerful framework for success in business. This integration is not a one-time exercise but a continuous journey of refinement and growth. Don't stop.

THE IMPORTANCE OF CONDUCTING BUSINESS THROUGH A PLACE OF STRATEGY, NOT EMOTION

In the dynamic and competitive landscape of the business world, decisions are the currency of success. Every choice made by a business leader has the potential to shape the destiny of the organization. In this chapter, we explore the critical distinction between conducting business through a place of strategy versus a place of emotion and underscore the significance of rational decision-making in fostering long-term success.

It took a long time for me to see how my emotions and ego stopped me from growing. While emotions are an inherent part of the human experience, and business leaders are not exempt from their influence, they are able to box them up and put them aside when they get in the way. It is natural for emotions to overflow in response to success, failure, or the pressure of competition. However, the challenge lies in not allowing these emotions to cloud judgment when making crucial business decisions. This is where mindfulness and self-awareness are the most needed.

Decisions made under the influence of fleeting emotions may yield immediate satisfaction but often prove detrimental overall. Leaders who prioritize emotional satisfaction over strategic thinking risk compromising the stability and sustainability of their businesses. You must, at all times, be rational.

Conducting business through a place of strategy involves a disciplined and rational approach to decision-making. Strategic decisions are founded on a comprehensive understanding of the market, industry trends, and the organization's capabilities. Rational decision-making transcends momentary emotions, focusing instead on the alignment of choices with overarching business goals. I am not saying you should not trust your gut, you should, but do not let personal emotions drown out your strategic thinking.

A strategic mindset encourages leaders to look beyond immediate gains and losses. Instead of reacting impulsively to short-term market fluctuations or emotional pressures, a strategic approach involves considering the long-term implications of each decision. This not only ensures the sustainability of the business but also contributes to the development of a resilient and adaptable organization.

Emotional decision-making often leads to a neglect of risk assessment and mitigation. Strategic decision-makers, on the other hand, meticulously analyze potential risks and devise proactive measures to navigate challenges. By addressing risks through a logical lens, businesses can minimize the impact of unforeseen events and maintain a steady course toward their objectives.

Strategic decision-making also demands an objective evaluation of available options. Rather than succumbing to personal biases or emotional attachments, Entrepreneurs must assess alternatives based on quantitative and qualitative data. This analytical approach enhances the probability of making informed decisions that benefit the organization, and that is the whole goal here!

While advocating for a strategic approach, it is essential to acknowledge the role of emotions in human decision-making. Emotions provide valuable insights into human experience and can serve as a guide, prompting leaders to explore underlying concerns or motivations. The key is to strike a balance, leveraging the strengths of both emotional intelligence and strategic thinking. Jumping off my soap box now so we can get to work!

QUIZ: HOW MINDFUL ARE YOU?

Question 1: Awareness of Breath
How often do you consciously pay attention to your breath throughout the day?
a) Rarely or never
b) Occasionally
c) Frequently
d) Almost constantly

Question 2: Present Moment Observation
When you eat a meal, how often do you savor each bite and fully engage in the sensory experience?
a) Rarely or never
b) Occasionally
c) Frequently
d) Almost always

Question 3: Technology Distraction
How often do you find yourself mindlessly scrolling through your phone or other electronic devices without a specific purpose?
a) Frequently
b) Occasionally
c) Rarely
d) Never

Question 4: Mindful Listening
When having a conversation, how often are you fully present and actively listening without thinking about what you'll say next?
a) Rarely or never
b) Occasionally
c) Frequently
d) Almost always

Question 5: Body Awareness
How often do you check in with your body and notice physical sensations, like tension or relaxation?
a) Rarely or never
b) Occasionally
c) Frequently
d) Almost constantly

Question 6: Gratitude Practice
How often do you take a moment to express gratitude for the positive aspects of your life?
a) Rarely or never
b) Occasionally
c) Frequently
d) Daily

Question 7: Mind-Wandering
How often do you find your mind wandering, thinking about past or future events, rather than being fully present in the current moment?
a) Frequently
b) Occasionally
c) Rarely
d) Never

Question 8: Mindful Breathing
How often do you intentionally take a few deep breaths to bring your attention back to the present moment?
a) Rarely or never
b) Occasionally
c) Frequently
d) Almost constantly

Scoring:

For each question, assign the following points based on the response:

a) Rarely or never = 1 point

b) Occasionally = 2 points

c) Frequently = 3 points

d) Almost constantly = 4 points

Your Results:

8-16 points: You may benefit from incorporating more mindfulness practices into your daily life.

17-24 points: You have a moderate level of mindfulness, but there's room for improvement.

25-32 points: You demonstrate a high level of mindfulness and presence in your daily activities.

Write down three goals right now. Hopefully one of them is to be more mindful! Okay, enough of the warm and fluffy stuff. Let's get going!

CHAPTER 3:

BUSINESS BASICS YOU NEED TO KNOW

E ducate yourself. You do not need a college degree to be smart and having one does not make you smart either. Education is not just a formal process, so even if you have a degree in something, that does not mean you know about business. My parents both had only earned a high school diploma and they ran many successful businesses throughout my life. They were entrepreneurial in every way and educated themselves with books, seminars, and by socializing with people in the fields of their businesses. But every entrepreneur must know the basics of business to succeed, no matter what space he or she is in as an inventor, investor, salesperson, or professional. You cannot build something with growth potential without a solid foundation. So many new businesses do not make it past the first year because of a lack of foundation, structure, business systems, and leadership.

Start off right with a solid foundation. Choose your business structure correctly. Have all your legal documents and agreements organized. Choose your accounting system smartly. Automate what you can. Keep your overhead low. Be a leader and know your weaknesses. Your biggest strength should be knowing what you are NOT great at so you can hire someone to assist in that area.

Eventually, you will likely need to talk to an attorney and an accountant. Try to find an attorney who is well-versed in corporate law and employment law. Some attorneys offer prepaid monthly packages for businesses that don't need a full-time general counsel.

An accountant is important to help you avoid tax implications, help you set up your preferred accounting method, and assist in quarterly reporting. You cannot control what you cannot measure and see; an accounting professional gives you the ability to measure and control.

There are some basic terms and concepts you need to know.

Accounts Receivable
This is money coming in! Money owed to you by your customers. It is also a tangible asset!

Accounts Payable
This is money you must pay to survive. These are your costs and expenses for everything.

Assets
Assets are the tangible and intangible things owned by a company that have value. Tangible assets are physical things that can be sold to force a company to pay its debts. This can include inventory, cash, stocks, bonds, equipment, computers, cars, furniture, and the company's account receivables.

Intangible assets are things with no physical presence, such as goodwill, brand recognition, patents, trademarks, and copyrights.

B2B
B2B is short code for Business to Business. It means that your customer is another business.

B2C
B2C is short code for Business to Consumer. It means that your customer is a consumer or a real person.

Cash Flow
Cash flow is the total amount of money moving in and out of your business and is an indicator of the company's liquidity or lack thereof.

Cost of Goods Sold (COGS)
COGS are the directs costs that can be attributed to the production of the things your company sells.

Expenses
Simply put, it is the "cost" of operating a business. Expenses are the money you spend on everything to operate the business. This includes rent, wages, insurance, furniture, marketing, advertising, materials, staff, and business services.

Fixed Costs
Fixed costs are all the overhead costs that you must pay every month, whether your business makes money or not. This is your rent, your utilities, salaries for your employees and business equipment expenses. I call these the profit eaters. Keep these low.

Gross Profit
Gross profit is revenue minus the cost of goods sold (COGS), which again are the direct costs that come from the production

of the goods sold in the company. This includes materials and wages you must pay the workers that make the product.

Liabilities

Liabilities are the things that the company is responsible for, such as debts, wages that are owed, money owed to suppliers, money owed to vendors, money owed for rent, outstanding taxes, bank debt, and any other kind of financial obligation.

Net Profit

Net profit is also called the bottom line. This is the money left over after paying for all expenses, debts, additional income streams, and operating costs.

Net Operating Loss

When the company's expenses exceed the **income** or total revenue produced in a specific time period. Businesses that have a **net loss** don›t have to go bankrupt because they can use their retained earnings or loans to stay afloat until a profit is earned. This is important because, as an entrepreneur, you may not turn a profit in the first year.

The formula is Revenues – Expenses = Net Profit or Net Loss

Let's say you sell 10,000 widgets for $1 each this year, generating an annual revenue of $10,000. To operate the business, you needed to pay $20,000 this year to purchase materials to make the widgets and pay its employees. (That is COGS and operating expenses, see how it all works?)

$$\$10,000–\$20,000 = \$10,000$$

Because the company paid more in expenses than it earned in revenue for the year, it suffered a net loss of $10,000.

Operating Expenses

Operating expenses are all the costs NOT related to the product of goods, such as your rent, utility bills, water and coffee service, paper products, and legal costs.

Profit Margin

The profit margin is the amount of revenue from sales that exceeds the costs of your company. To determine your profit margin, you first need to know what your gross profit is. Once you have calculated that, divide the **gross profit** by the revenue. To make the **margin** a percentage, multiply the result by 100.

For example, you sell Widgets for $200 each. Each widget costs you $150 to make. So, to find your gross profit, find the difference between the revenue ($200) and the cost ($150). (COGS, remember! You're really catching on here!)

So, $200 − $150 = $50 gross profit

To find the margin, divide gross profit by the revenue.

$50 / $200 = 0.25 margin

To make the margin a percentage, multiply the result by 100.

0.25 X 100 = 25% margin

The margin is 25%. That means you keep 25% of your total revenue. You spent the other 75% making your widgets! The greater the margin, the more money you keep. This number is an indication of the value of your company! Cut costs and your margin will be higher.

Return on Investment (ROI)
Return on investment (ROI) is called a performance measure. This number is used to see if the investment is "worth it." The calculation is easy, you simply divide the amount of money you made from the investment (what you received) by the cost of the investment (what you spent).

Revenue
Revenue is the total amount of income generated by the sale of all goods and services that come directly from the company's primary business. Revenue is a raw number that does not consider all the expenses that still need to be paid.

Supply and Demand
In economics, "supply and demand" is the direct relationship between the quantity (availability) of a product and the number of people who want to buy it. This is the main economic theory used to determine prices. If you have 100 products and 1000 people who want to buy them, logically, you can charge a lot more than if you have 100 products and 2 people who want to buy them.

Variable Costs
These are the expenses that ebb and flow with your business activities. If you are a restaurateur, the more patrons you have the more food and wine you need to buy. Hence, there is a direct relation to your expenses and volume.

BEFORE YOU START, DO THIS FIRST
The purpose of this next section is just to get these items on your radar before you move forward. These concepts are all explained in the following chapters, but I wanted you to keep these ideas in the front of your mind while you are reading and preparing to launch.

Before you name your business and file for your incorporation, do a trademark search to make sure are not inadvertently stealing someone else's idea, concept, or name. Google it, check social media, and make sure you are all clear for takeoff.

1. If you have content that is unique and proprietary, file for a copyright. If your business logo or name is unique, you may want to consider filing for a trademark or service mark before you launch. Write down the date you first used the idea, concept, slogan, logo, or name because you will need that for your application. Keep copies of all social media posts in a paper folder as well as a digital folder so you have that for your applications.

2. If you are hiring people to help you, make them sign a Confidentiality and Non-Compete Agreement before you tell them your idea or before you share any trade secrets or proprietary information.

3. Make sure you understand the basics of a profit and loss statement. Learn how to read one so you can always keep your company's economic growth on your radar.

4. Understand how fixed and variable costs affect your business. Do not take on too much from the onset; it is far easier to add things than to get out of contracts later. Before you commit to ANYTHING that is a fixed cost, research all your options as far as purchasing, leasing, and even outsourcing. Do not hire too many people up front, start slowly, maybe even part time or independent contractors until you're certain that there is enough work to justify and compensate for the expense.

5. At all times, without exception, you need to be aware of how your fixed and variable expenses impact your revenue. The only way to justify and overcome your fixed costs is to have enough business volume to absorb them. The more fixed expenses you have, the more business you need to do, which then increases your variable expenses. It is circuitous, I know, but that is how it works.

6. Know the difference between equity financing and debt financing.

7. Understand the legal and regulatory requirements of your type of business and industry. Make sure you have all the required licenses and insurance.

Homework: (Yep, homework!) Study these terms and concepts and learn them solidly. Write a two-paragraph synopsis of your business idea and use as many, if not all, of the concepts above. If you think they do not apply, use a "pivot" idea, and figure out how to work it into your idea. Give yourself 1 point for every term you use.

Grade Yourself

15 and above:	Well done! You are serious about becoming an entrepreneur.
10–14:	Great job! You are well on your way to becoming an entrepreneur.
7–13:	Good job, but you could try harder.
6 or below:	Shaking my head. Just no. Go back and try again.

CHAPTER 4:

THE IDEA

The primary driving force for inventing something is "need." Problems NEED solutions. Look at problems as exciting opportunities for new products or services to develop. As the great Greek philosopher Plato said, "*Our need will be the real creator*," and of course the old proverb "*Necessity is the mother of invention*." Sometimes ideas are money makers, and sometimes they are complete failures.

Mostly, Entrepreneurs do not just suddenly appear and start making millions. They are often people who work in an industry and start recognizing the gaps in the market, where one product ends and other begins and the space in between that needs to be filled by an innovative idea. But let's face it; how many innovative ideas are there really? Not that many; so, it will come down to timing, adjustments, marketing, and need. Here is the best part: You do not need to produce a new idea; you do not need to invent anything! All you need to do is to find the gap in the market where a problem needs a solution.

Sometimes entrepreneurs are educated people who after years of working in an industry, such as technology, develop a keen idea of how solutions can also create problems, so another solution may be needed. They have an awareness and an openness to be a little disruptive and unconventional. They really do think outside the box.

Some qualities are inherent, and some can be learned; everyone has different talents and learning how to compensate for your weaknesses is how you will develop the right skill set. The skill set for that would be

1. Learn how to spot and identify problems.
2. Learn how to produce solutions to those problems.
3. Learn how to be forward thinking and adapt your idea as more problems arise.
4. Learn how to pivot when your target customer's needs change.
5. Learn how to recognize gaps in the market.
6. Learn how to produce ideas that cut corners and save people money.
7. Learn how to produce ideas that save people time.
8. Learn how to recognize where a need can be fulfilled.
9. Learn how to use emotion as a tool to sell.

HOW TO EVALUATE AN IDEA

Come up with an idea right now, even if you think it is something ridiculous. Think of something that the general public needs, anything. Grab your journal and get ready to sketch out your idea and see if it is ready to put into action. Follow the steps below to frame out a business idea.

Here is your starting punch list:

1. Write down your idea; a rough sketch of the concept is sufficient.
2. What problem does your product or service solve?
3. For whom does the idea solve a problem; who is your target customer?

4. What is the purpose of this product or service?
5. Is anyone else doing this right now? If so, can you do it better? Cheaper?
6. What is the median income of your targeted customer?
7. How much does your product or service cost to make or deliver?
8. At what price will your product or service be sold?
9. What is the gross profit? What is your net profit?

If your net profit is negative or small, your idea needs to be tweaked. Maybe your targeted customer cannot afford your product or service. But the idea is still an idea! Keep it and rework it later.

Do not toss out your ideas. Keep them all in one place because markets change, trends change, and sometimes the world changes. Sometimes the gap in the market changes too.

It is important to not get bogged down in "busy work" when trying to turn your idea into a business. When you are sketching out ideas, you need to consider a few things so your idea will evolve correctly.

Primarily, do not try to be too perfect when writing down your idea. As you go through the process, you will make changes and tweaks as necessary, so just sketch down a rough and raw version of whatever it was that hit you first. Do not let yourself get tangled up in the small stuff at this point or you will never get it off the metaphorical drawing board.

Second, do not be so hung up on this idea that you CANNOT change it when needed. Money, money, money. Focus! Focus!

Third, again, remember that this idea is supposed to make money. So do not put blinders on when considering the business model and business plan because you want to focus on the technical side or the production side of your idea. You need to follow the steps and ensure that this idea is worth the investment. You will not know if this idea is profitable unless you write it down and track it correctly.

Fourth, do not forget the most important person in this process: your customer (remember the money thing?) Do not focus on packaging, marketing, or competitors yet. Figure out who your customer is and tailor ALL of that around THEM.

Fifth, look at market trends, social trends, and world events. If you were opening a new type of business that focused on social gatherings while a pandemic was brewing, then you were not paying attention to timing, and you just lost all your seed money.

However, if you were focused on a business model that provided products to help businesses keep customers socially distant, then your timing would be impeccable.

Last, surround yourself with people who share or support your vision. You need a good team to help you get this idea off the ground, turn it into a product or service, and convert that to money in the bank.

If you follow these steps, and your idea is good, move on to the next steps. Execution and implementation.

If you have the money, you can hire a forecaster and do market research. Just remember your purpose, your customer, your money.

CHAPTER 5:

THE ACTION PLAN

We all have that friend that is always coming up with ideas for inventions and businesses. But how many businesses do they open? How many inventions do they patent? Getting an idea over the finish line is what makes you an entrepreneur—not just thinking like one.

Then there is the most unimaginative person on the planet who is a serial Entrepreneur opening business after business. That person knows the process of opening a business. Getting ideas over the finish line is the hard part and that process starts with an action plan.

Even if you have an established business, you still need an action plan in order to pivot when necessary or to take your business to new levels. If you are a licensed professional, you will also be accountable to regulatory agencies and must follow strict ethical codes and professional rules. All this needs to be written down and then "baked in" to your plans.

This can benefit both the large and small business owner. It is simply the strategy or course of action that you are going to take to get started.

An action plan, simply put, focuses on the right information in the right order. It organizes the "project" of creating a business. Certain things need to happen first, or your process will not flow correctly. Delays are always inevitable, but do not let them be your fault, and don't let them occur because of poor planning and lack of a timeline.

That is exactly what the action plan accomplishes, a checklist of steps to take to get your business off the ground. A lot of this seems repetitive, and it is to an extent, but that is a good thing. It will create a nice foundation on which to stack your building blocks. So, let's make a list of all the steps you need to take in order to achieve your goal. Use the method of what, why, where, who, and when to create your plan.

What? They are the objectives and goals of the action plan.

When? This represents your timeline of deadlines and dates and is your overall schedule.

Where? This is your logistics schedule. For example, applying for a license would occur at the governmental entity's building. Brainstorming may be at a meeting area; marketing research may be at a target research company office.

Who? This is your team and their assigned tasks.

How? This is the list of the stages of your project.

Why? Clearly define your product or service and explain what your business offers and what problems it solves for your targeted customer. Let's get granular.

1. WHAT ARE YOUR GOALS? ARE THEY MEASURABLE AND ACHIEVABLE?

You must create measurable goals.

Make a list of all the tasks you want to accomplish. Again, use the concepts of who, what, why, and when. Setting expectations is important and remember this will be your life for the next several months or years.

> **Sample 1:** "Obtain a liquor license and start a mobile bar that can be rented for parties. The bar will be made from a customized food truck and can be rented out for parties. The liquor license will take six months to obtain, and the food truck will be customized during that time. The license is $25,000 and the customization is $7,000. I plan to have the business open on or before January 1, 2020, and book at least two parties the first month, three parties the second month, and then four parties per month thereafter. After two years, the plan is to add two new mobile bars per year."

> **Sample 2:** To buy an already profitable business and hire a manager to run the entire enterprise. Use a business broker and pay a commission to ensure I get a profitable business and that due diligence is done correctly.

> **Sample 3:** To build three e-commerce stores by myself and add a new store every quarter.

The above samples illustrate that objectives are subjective (*yes, let that marinate until you think "ohhhhhh yeah"*). Why are they so subjective? Because everyone is different and how they define success is different too. Some people are driven solely by revenue, and others define success by building an empire that helps people and makes their brand a household name. You need to consider where you are now, where you want to go, and what fuels the engine that will get you there. This is largely a personality decision.

I had a former client who owns a special kind of movie theater (yup), and he picks up bags of money on Monday morning. He never steps foot into the business. He has no interaction with clients, customers, or employees. On the other end of the spectrum, I have another client who owns a retail store and goes to work every single day because she loves helping people pick out outfits. She loves working with vendors and deciding trends; she made a life out of this. She makes quite a bit of money and doesn't have to go to the store, but her love of clothes and people is also a big draw for the store. She was driven by lifestyle and joy, whereas the former client was driven by bags of money and sitting in his pool all day. She was driven by the activity, and he was driven by freedom.

How do you know if your business idea will be successful? You won't if it is not measurable. This is done by data gathering with respect to revenue, competition, market research group analysis, and even social media campaigns that provide analytics.

Another consideration is making sure to account for lifetime value and longevity. You must plan for growth and expansion. Do you have a concept that can pivot if the economy crashes or trends change and force you out of business?

This is another way to get a quick snapshot of how measurable your idea is by determining a basic revenue. I call this a mini development plan. This is how I sketch out rough ideas. Keep in mind that this has various goods and services on it to give everyone an idea, but this type of plan would be about one single entity and similar services and products.

Start a spreadsheet and input all the goods and services that you plan to sell. Next, input the cost of the goods and services to you. Then, input the price you intend to charge. Add how many you intend to sell per quarter or annually. Don't worry about all the other expenses yet, that will come later. Now evaluate the anticipated revenue after taking away the cost to purchase the item. This is just a tiny snapshot to see if you are choosing products or services that will give you a big enough profit margin. It does not consider overhead expenses, fulfillment costs, or other costs of getting the product to the consumer.

GOODS/SERVICES	PRICE PER UNIT	TARGETED ANNUAL SALES GOALS	COST	YOUR RETAIL PRICE POINT	REVENUE GENERATED	ANTICIPATED ADJUSTED REVENUE
Litigation Services	0	2000 billable hours	0	$550.00 per hour	$1,100,000.00	$1,100,000.00
Flat Fee Legal Services	$100.00	240	$100 PER HOUR FOR PARALEGAL	$450.00	$112,500.00	$88,500.00
Consultation Services	0	2000 hours	0	$250.00 per hour	$500,000.00	$500,000.00
Sunglasses	$5.00/unit	1000 units	$5000.00	35.00	$35,000.00	$30,000.00
Leather Bound Journals	$20.00/unit	1000 units	$20,000.00	$45.00	$45,000	$25.000.00
Exercise resistance Bands	$5.00/unit	1000 units	$5000.00	35.00	$35,000.00	$30,000.00
Credit Card Protector	$5.00/unit	1000 units	$5000.00	35.00	$35,000.00	$30,000.00
Face Masks/pack of 5	$5.00/unit	1000 units	$5000.00	35.00	$35,000.00	$30,000.00
TOTALS:			$40,000 cash on the street, $24,000 to be paid for services when rendered			Anticipated revenue: 1, 833, 500,00

2. IDENTIFY THE MEMBERS OF YOUR ACTION PLAN GROUP

This is your brainstorming success squad. It can include your attorney, test marketers, social media e-commerce specialists, business partners, and investors. Each party will be assigned a role and specific tasks. This is your "who."

3. MAKE A LIST OF ALL TASKS

Under each task, provide the details as to who will complete the task, the expected completion date, alternative actions if the task cannot be completed, if there is a deadline, and all activities that are required to complete the task. Sample items would be obtaining any licenses needed, obtaining insurance, incorporating the business, getting an EIN, hiring a web designer, leasing a space, creating marketing materials, writing a business plan, developing a business model, finding investors, and planning your grand opening. Make sure each task has a deadline and an alternate action. Make sure you start with the tasks that may take the longest first, like obtaining a license or leasing a space. This is your "who," your "when," and your "where."

4. CREATE A VISION BOARD

One of the most important things you can do for yourself, and your team, is to create a board so you can SEE your accomplishments and track your progress. Update this board regularly. Meet as often as you can, even if it is just a group chat or a Zoom call. Touch base and keep everything up to date and ensure that you have all the tasks organized so that they are occurring sequentially, and you will not have any delays. This is your "when" and your "how." Communication is key and this will require you to be on top of the project and your people. Keep your project organized, updated, accessible to the team, and visible to all.

How did you do? This chapter was a lot of work, but you are literally building your business one chapter at a time.

Check in with yourself and see how you are feeling mentally. Do you feel excited and encouraged? Or do you feel overwhelmed and uninspired?

Do not get discouraged; it is a lot of work to build a business and maybe your idea is not inspiring you or maybe you need to take a break for a day or two and see how you feel.

Get in touch with your inner purpose and see if you are straying from it or nurturing it.

Your homework: Come up with your own catchphrase to say to yourself when you need to be reminded of why you are doing this. What is your motivation?

1. **I want freedom.**
2. **I want to be helpful.**
3. **I want to be well-known.**
4. **I want to be a social media influencer.**
5. **I want to be respected**
6. **I want to be different**
7. **I want to be filthy rich (hey, that is OKAY!!!)**

Breathe. Relax. Rest. And get ready to draft your very own business plan.

CHAPTER 6:

THE BUSINESS PLAN

All great business plans have one thing in common, regardless of the industry. Do you know what that is? **SIMPLICITY**. An effective business plan is a living document; meaning it will change, expand and contract according to your business needs. The second thing all great business plans have in common is clarity—get to the point fast so the reader immediately sees your idea and value. This is a big picture document, so take caution to not get tangled up in too many details.

There are fixed components to a business plan. Some plans are more complex and others less complicated. For example, if you are trying to attract investors or trying to secure a bank loan, you may need more, or maybe less, detail.

1. EXECUTIVE SUMMARY
Even though is number one, this is the section you should do last because it summarizes the entire business plan. It should be a brief and comprehensive overview of the business plan.

2. COMPANY DESCRIPTION
Use this section to describe what your company has to offer, how it differs from other similar companies. What is your purpose and company statement? What separates you from the competition? Highlight your strengths.

3. MANAGEMENT TEAM

Who are you and what are your qualifications? What are you all about? Are you a serial entrepreneur with a history of success or a first-time entrepreneur with a strong educational background or experience in the industry? What sparked your business idea—a life event or years in an industry? How is your company organized and who are your executive team members? Don't be afraid to toot your own horn.

4. PRODUCT OR SERVICE

What are you selling? That is the obvious starting place. But don't forget to include what problem your product solves, why it is unique, or what will make it sell better than any other similar product. Include its basic characteristics and describe it in such a way that the reader understands exactly what you are trying to sell.

5. TARGET MARKET AND MARKET ANALYSIS

You created a product or a service or built this business idea around it so certainly you know who needs it. Think hard; what problem does this solve and who will use it? Who needs it the most? Are there any other products on the market that are similar? Take that a few steps further and this is called market analysis. How old is your target consumer? Where do they live? What are the demographics? Does the geography or locale provide any benefits to hardships to getting your product to the consumer? Are there any cultural considerations? In this section, include a brief business development plan. In that plan, include any competitors in your targeted area.

6. DISTRIBUTION AND MARKETING

This is where you will discuss price, distribution/fulfillment, and marketing strategies.

Where is your largest reach? If your targeted consumer is on social media, then that is where you should focus your marketing strategies. How will you get your product and service to the consumer? Digital delivery? Face-to-face service? Drop ship from a manufacturer? This should all be outlined in this section. Also include how the unique features of your service or product sets you apart from your competitors.

Publicity helps—think of what tactics you can afford to employ. Can you hire a public relations firm? Will you take out print advertisements? SEO marketing strategies?

7. FINANCE AND BUDGET: EQUITY CAPITAL, PERSONAL CONTRIBUTIONS, SEED MONEY, LOANS, AND FINANCING

How much money do you need to start and where is it coming from? How much capital will keep in reserve? How much money comes from personal finances? Do you need to budget for employees for your own living expenses? Do you have current or prospective loans? Start off by detailing how much money you need, how much money you have, what you think you will need in the future, and your plans for where all the funds will come from. Equity capital is one component of the finance plan. Banks and financiers will want to know how much capital came from your own personal resources, so make sure to log that separately. All financing should be described here. Next, you want to list all the operating expenses and costs for starting up, production, payroll, licensing fees, etc.

Include what projected sales you are aiming for and what you think they will be in each of your market segments.

8. LEGAL FORM OF YOUR CHOSEN ENTITY

Your business plan should also contain explanations about the chosen legal form of the company. Which person or other corporation(s) holds a part of the company? Why did you choose this form of legal entity? Will the entity become part of a hierarchy of parent or subsidiary companies in the future?

Do not confuse a business plan with a business model. You need both, you may not need either. Of course, it is ideal to have both, but many successful people have done fine without them. If you are looking for financing, such as a small business loan, they will likely require a business plan.

So, let's talk about a business model as compared to the business plan, as it is a concept you should know and understand.

WHAT IS A BUSINESS MODEL?

A general description of a business model is a design for the successful operation of a business that identifies revenue sources, identifies a solid customer base, identifies the retail or commercial products or services, and identifies the details of financing. Simply put, it is how you plan to make your money. That's it.

However, oversimplifying is not always the best idea; so, while the concept may be simple, the business model itself requires some key components to make sense. Those key components should include target customers, the market, organization strengths and challenges, the essential elements of your service or product, and how it will be sold.

While there are many different business models, there are four basic structures, such as manufacturer, distributor, retailer, and franchise. Each category will have subcategories, such as retailer can be broken down into e-commerce, drop shipper, or affiliate. Franchise can be broken down into licensee, and then, of course, we also have professionals like doctors, lawyers, and health professionals, such as a registered nurse that operates a medical spa.

With all the competition out there, the business plan will clearly illustrate how your company can add value to the customer and profit from delivering the product or service. Basically, it should demonstrate logistically how your company is set apart from the competitor. Think of a business model as a conceptual "sketch" of how your business will operate. It is quite different from a business plan and is more of an operational structure and should answer the following questions.

What is your product or service?

1. How is your product or service differentiated in the market?
2. What is your product positioning? (How will you market it?)
3. What are your product challenges?
4. Who is your customer?
5. What are your customer challenges?
6. How should we research the customer?
7. How can you deliver your product or service to your customer?
8. How can you collect payment and how will you profit from that?
9. How can the company continue to grow?
10. What is the company vision?
11. How adaptable is your product or service if trends change?

12. Share your business plan and business model with your friends and family; ask for feedback. Leave your ego behind though because, remember, they are also consumers, and they will give you honest feedback.

Your goal is to make money, not friends. Your goal is to be successful, not revered as a genius.

Your goal is to make money, not be the only one who worked to hone this idea. Now, the next step is the most exciting because things are about to get real. It is official once you incorporate!

PART TWO:

SET!

CHAPTER 7:

HOW TO CHOOSE THE RIGHT BUSINESS ENTITY

By nature, an entrepreneur is a disruptor, breaking through norms and going his or her own way to pursue a passion. So now you must make a decision that puts you right back in the box you broke free from. (Oh, f*&!). You may want to rebel, but that is not what this is about. This is part of the game you must play, so get your head straight about having to put your magnificent self back into this box because this is the first and most weighty decision you will make as business owner. It is a small but important corporate box with structure and regulations. Hey, it's ok! Put on your thinking cap and ask yourself, "***What type of business entity do I need***?" This is the vehicle in which you will travel to reach your ultimate destination: outrageously big and bodacious freaking success.

Which entity you choose will be determined by what your needs and wants are, so take some notes. First, look at other companies in your industry. I bet most of them have chosen the same entity type. Each structure provides unique benefits and liabilities. Let's focus on five different corporate structures, considering legal liability, costs, taxes, and flexibility.

CHOOSING YOUR BUSINESS STRUCTURE

Again, in perusing the right business structure for your business, consider what other small businesses in your field are doing. For example, technology companies will typically have different structures compared to a law firm. While better understanding your field will help in the decision-making process, each business is unique with diverse needs. You will also want to understand the following factors and how they may impact your business:

- Legal liability
- Costs
- Taxes
- Flexibility
- The future needs of your company

Next, let's look at the most prominent structures available.

SOLE PROPRIETORSHIP

Sole proprietorships are the easiest businesses to form, and they give the owner complete control of the company. Any organization is automatically considered sole proprietorship if the owner doesn't register as otherwise. This is typically the most cost efficient when starting out.

In this case, the personal assets and liabilities go together with business ones when it comes to taxes. So, the owner can be held accountable for the debts and obligations of the company. As the company grows, so does the potential legal liability of the owner.

PARTNERSHIPS

If two or more people own a company together, they form a partnership. Two prominent types of such organizations are limited and limited liability.

In limited partnerships, only one partner has unlimited liability. Other partners have limited liability as well as limited control over business operations.

The latter kind is similar. The main difference is that every owner has limited liability. That way, all partners have protection from the partnership's debts, and they're not responsible for the activities of other associates.

LIMITED LIABILITY COMPANY (LLC)

LLCs allow owners to enjoy the benefits of both corporations and partnerships. They protect from personal liability and avoid corporate taxes by taxing company revenue through personal income statements. The only catch is that members must pay self-employment taxes.

If you decide to form an LLC, remember that they have limited life in many states. In some cases, every time a member joins or leaves it, you need to dissolve and reform it.

A limited liability company (LLC) is a business structure allowed by state statute. Each state may use different regulations, you should check with your state if you are interested in starting a limited liability company.

Owners of an LLC are called members. Most states do not restrict ownership, so members may include individuals, corporations, other LLCs, and foreign entities. There is no maximum number of members. Most states also permit "single member" LLCs, those having only one owner.

A few types of businesses generally cannot be LLCs, such as banks and insurance companies. Check your state's requirements and the federal tax regulations for further information. And to further complicate it, there are special rules for foreign LLCs.

CLASSIFICATIONS

Depending on elections made by the LLC and the number of members, the IRS will treat an LLC as either a corporation, partnership, or as part of the LLC's owner's tax return (a "disregarded entity"). Specifically, a domestic LLC with at least two members is classified as a partnership for federal income tax purposes unless it files Form 8832 and affirmatively elects to be treated as a corporation. For income tax purposes, an LLC with only one member is treated as an entity disregarded as separate from its owner unless it files Form 8832 and elects to be treated as a corporation. However, for the purposes of employment tax and certain excise taxes, an LLC with only one member is still considered a separate entity.

CORPORATIONS

In general, these entities offer a high level of protection for their owners. However, this feature comes at a high cost, with many fees and a lot of paperwork.

There are five main types of corporations. Below, we'll take a quick glance at them.

- **C Corps** are legal entities separate from their owners. They can earn a profit, pay taxes, and be liable legally. C corps pay income tax for their revenue and have a separate life from shareholders.
- **S Corps** have the goal of avoiding double taxation of regular corporations. Some losses and profits can pass through the owners› income statements without becoming subject to corporate tax. This structure also comes with several limitations.
- **B Corps** or "benefit corporations" are different from regular corps in purpose and transparency, but not in taxes. Their focus is both mission and profit, producing a public benefit as well as financial gains.
- **Close corporations** are like B corps, but with a less traditional structure. The shares can't get traded publicly, and shareholders run such entities without the need for a board of directors.
- **Nonprofit corporations** do charity, educational, literary, scientific, and religious work. They get tax exemptions because their work benefits the public, which means they don›t pay income taxes. Other rules for organization are the same as with a regular corporation.

Choosing the appropriate corporate structure is a super critical decision for entrepreneurs and business owners. There are many considerations before you create your entity because it could affect long term growth and the ability to raise capital. While both C and S corporations offer unique advantages and disadvantages, they exhibit fundamental differences that influence decision-making for entrepreneurs and business owners, so refer to the questionnaire below to assess your specific needs (this is not legal advice! Please seek the advice of your own tax or legal professional).

TAXATION:

S Corporation: One of the primary distinctions between S corps and C corps lies in their taxation methods. S corporations employ a pass-through taxation model. This means that the corporation itself does not pay federal income taxes. Instead, profits and losses are "passed through" to the shareholders, who report them on their individual tax returns. This structure effectively eliminates the potential for double taxation.

C Corporation: In contrast, C corporations face a system of double taxation. They are taxed at the corporate level on their profits, and when dividends are distributed to shareholders, those dividends are taxed again at the individual level. While this structure provides the advantage of retained earnings for reinvestment, it can lead to higher overall tax liability.

OWNERSHIP AND SHAREHOLDERS:

S Corporation: S corporations are subject to restrictions on ownership and shareholders. They are limited to 100 shareholders or fewer, and only individuals, estates, specific trusts, and certain tax-exempt organizations are eligible to be shareholders. Non-U.S. citizens/residents, corporations, and partnerships are ineligible.

C Corporation: C corporations offer more flexibility in terms of ownership. They have no limitations on the number or type of shareholders they can have. This allows for diverse ownership structures, making C corps an attractive option for larger enterprises or those seeking investment from a wide range of sources.

MANAGEMENT AND STRUCTURE:

S Corporation: S corporations typically maintain a more informal and adaptable management structure. They are managed by a board of directors and officers, providing flexibility in decision-making processes.

C Corporation: C corporations follow a more formalized structure with a board of directors, officers, and shareholders. This structured approach is designed to ensure transparent governance and reporting practices.

CAPITAL RAISING:

S Corporation: Due to the limitations on ownership and shareholders, S corporations may face challenges in raising capital. Their options for attracting external investment are more restricted.

C Corporation: C corporations excel in capital-raising endeavors. They have the ability to issue different classes of stock with varying voting rights, which can be highly appealing to potential investors.

1. **What are your long-term business goals?**
   - Consider your growth plans, potential exit strategies, and whether you plan to go public in the future.

2. **How many shareholders do you plan to have?**
   - C corporations can have an unlimited number of shareholders, while S corporations are limited to 100 shareholders.

3. **Do you want to have different classes of stock?**
   - C corporations can have multiple classes of stock, while S corporations can only have one class of stock.

4. **Do you want foreign shareholders or non-individual shareholders (like other corporations or LLCs)?**
   - S corporations have restrictions on who can be a shareholder, while C corporations do not.

5. **What is your preferred tax treatment?**
   - C corporations are subject to double taxation (corporate and individual levels), while S corporations pass through income to shareholders, avoiding double taxation.

6. **Do you anticipate significant profits early on?**
   - S corporations can be advantageous for startups with expected losses in the early years because they can pass through those losses to the individual shareholders.

7. **Are you concerned about personal liability protection?**
   - Both C and S corporations provide limited liability protection, but it's important to consult with legal counsel to understand the specifics.

8. **How do you plan to compensate owners and employees?**
   - Consider how you want to structure salaries, bonuses, and benefits, as this can have tax implications for both C and S corporations.

9. **What industry is your business in?**
   - Some industries may have specific regulatory considerations that could influence your choice of corporate structure.

10. **Do you plan to reinvest profits into the business or distribute them to shareholders?**
    - C corporations may have more flexibility in retaining earnings for growth, while S corporations pass through profits directly to shareholders.

11. **Are you willing to comply with additional administrative requirements for an S corporation?**
    - S corporations have stricter eligibility requirements and additional administrative obligations compared to C corporations.

12. **Have you consulted with a tax advisor or legal counsel? (You know I have to say this).**
    - It is so important I to seek professional advice from a tax advisor or attorney who is familiar with your specific situation and can provide personalized guidance. Everyone's situation is different, so do not listen to your friends either.

MEET THE PARENTS: CORPORATIONS AND THEIR SUBSIDIARIES

Revenue and the Subsidiary

Is your company set up using a parent-subsidiary structure? It can be a beneficial arrangement that helps a business owner reduce certain risks with respect to various ventures. The caveat is that managing businesses is more complicated than owning each business in an individual capacity. The subsidiary's profits must go through the parent company before any of the cash ends up in your pocket.

What is the Parent-Subsidiary Relationship?

First, what is a subsidiary? A subsidiary is a corporation or limited liability company that is owned by another company, which is called the parent. Usually, the parent is structured as a C corporation, but it can also be another LLC. Sometimes the parent owns 100 percent of the subsidiary, and other times it just owns the majority interest.

Why would I need a subsidiary?

Serial entrepreneurs have one thing more than anyone in the world: ideas. One reason a subsidiary is utilized is because it maintains a separate identity between the parent company brands. So, if you have a corporation, and do not want to water down the new or existing brand, the subsidiary is an obvious choice. Think of certain high-end cosmetic brands, like Yves Saint Laurent. How would people feel spending $38 on a tube of lipstick if the new product were owned by L'Oréal, who sells an economy brand lipstick for $4.99? Why would anyone spend an extra $33? Brand. Marketing. Goodwill. Packaging. To elaborate on goodwill, it is the most unique intangible asset a company owns. A subsidiary allows a brand to create and maintain that unique good will.

Another reason a subsidiary is created is to facilitate an acquisition when the acquiring entity intends to keep the acquired company's name and culture. It tips customers off that substantial changes are coming and can affect the revenue stream. Subsidiaries can also help you posture your business as an alternative to the parent company at a different price point. Consider the luxury brands that own separate lower value brands. There are many reasons, such as taxes and finances also.

Distributing Profits

Profit—that is the whole point to you becoming an entrepreneur! The word profit means a financial gain, specifically the difference between the amount earned and the amount spent in buying, operating, or producing something. Most businesses manage finances annually by deducting expenses from revenue to determine the net income. Then, taxes are paid on net income; after the taxes are paid on the net income, BAM! That is your profit. Profits are then distributed to the owners and the board of directors can vote to distribute all or a portion of the company's profits to shareholders as dividends. An LLC will distribute profits to members based on the way the company has chosen to be taxed.

Parent Companies as Owners

How the subsidiary is organized, meaning whether it is an LLC or corporation, is of no consequence to the fact that the parent is its owner. The parent is either the sole (or majority) shareholder or member and is entitled to profit distributions from the subsidiary. The parent has control over the decision to distribute the subsidiary's profits. If the subsidiary is a corporation, the parent-shareholder gets to select the board members who make the decision regarding dividend distributions. Likewise, if the subsidiary is set up as an LLC, the parent controls who is hired to run the company's day-to-day operations.

Timing of Distributions

It is up to the subsidiary to decide the timing of dividend payments, such as paying them quarterly. There is no rule that states they must wait for year-end to distribute profits to its parent. One benefit of organizing your subsidiary as an LLC is that it can make a distribution on any reasonable schedule. And distributions can be based on profit projections.

Cautionary Considerations

If you have organized your subsidiary as an LLC, the tax elections will determine how the profits flow to the parent. If the LLC subsidiary is wholly owned by a single corporate parent, then the Internal revenue Service will categorize it as a single-member LLC. And, if the single-member LLC elects to be taxed as a disregarded entity, the profits and losses will be passed through to the parent instead of being reported by the subsidiary. LLC subsidiaries that elect status as disregarded entities are treated as a division of the parent for tax-reporting purposes. As such, the parent has more direct access to the subsidiary's profits.

The most utilized business structure is the corporation, but limited liability companies come in at a close second. LLCs are popular because they not only provide additional tax deductions and personal liability protection, but without the stringent administrative oversight requirements. Like all for-profit businesses, LLCs exist to make money for their owners. How an LLC claims its profits or losses depends on the status the LLC elects for tax purposes.

LLC–Articles of Organization

LLCs are created by filing articles of organization with the secretary of state. Owners of LLCs are called members. All states permit multimember LLCs, however there are some states that do not allow single-member LLCs. Keep in mind, an LLC is a blend of a partnership and a corporation. The LLC is like a corporation because it shares the same perpetual existence and is shielded from liability, but operationally and liability shielding like a corporation, but its operational and administrative flexibility mimics a partnership.

LLC Profit and Loss Statement

Sales, expenses, profits, and losses that a company generates during a specific period, often a month or a year will comprise the income statement. Although the income statement shows your LLC's financial performance, the company "claims" its profits or losses on its tax return.

Sole Proprietor

Sole proprietors are required to complete Schedule C, D, or E on their personal tax returns, Form 1040. Single member LLCs claim profits and losses on one of those schedules. When a single member does not elect tax treatment as a corporation, it will default to "disregarded entity" status. And, because a disregarded entity is treated as if a separate legal entity does not exist, then the single member LLC is treated as a sole proprietor.

General Partnership

A multimember LLC defaults to a general partnership for tax treatment as a. Multimember LLCs must complete Form 1065, partnership tax return and show profits and losses on this return. Multimember LLCs with partnership status must also complete Schedule K, which attributes the LLC's profits or losses to its members and provides each member with a copy of Schedule K-1. Members then claim their proportionate share of the LLC's profits and losses on their personal tax returns.

Corporation

A single member and multiple member LLC must elect tax treatment as a corporation by filing form 8832. An LLC taxed as corporations use Form 1120, corporation tax return, to claim profits and losses. Corporations pay taxes at the corporate level, so LLCs that are treated as corporations do the same.

General Partnership

A general partnership is created when two or more people join forces and finance and operate a business for profit. Remember, "people" can be individuals, limited liability companies, or corporations. However, each partner is responsible for the actions of the partnership, including profits and losses. You don't need a formal agreement to form a partnership, but it is most prudent to have a signed agreement that clearly dictates the responsibilities and contributions of each partner.

Explanation of "Flow Through" Profits

Partners in a general partnership receive "flow through" profits and report them on individual tax returns. Partners can share equally or have profits divided according to a partnership agreement. Even though the partners report the flow through profits on their individual tax returns, the partnership entity still must file an "information return" that reflects the showing income, deductions, profits, and losses on Form 1065. But this is NOT a tax return.

These concepts can be tricky. Do not hesitate to hire an attorney, business consultant, accountant, or manager to assist you with these tasks.

Getting Ready to Incorporate

In order to file for a new business, you will go to your state's Department of State Division of Corporations. You can do this online or mail in forms and documents, depending on your state. You can pay a third party to do it, or hire a lawyer, if you feel you do not understand what you need to do. If you're new to this, hire an attorney. The third-party companies on the internet charge a lot and cannot give you legal advice.

But before you incorporate your entity, you will need to draft your corporate governance documents. You will need these documents for a few reasons, such to open a business bank account, merchant accounts and to secure financing.

If you have partners or investors, the documents establish the rules about how the business will be managed as well as clearly define the rights and obligations of the owners.

As an entrepreneur, you may be inclined to skip this step or not take the documents seriously; you may trust that your partner won't hurt you or turn on you; but money can tear apart the closest of friendships and familial relationships. Expectations must be defined and managed, and these documents will do that. Having everything expressly memorialized in a document not only helps you if you get in a legal mess, but it also keeps people in check because there is no misinterpreting what the expectations are.

Since this is your first real step in making your business idea a reality, if you are using your own forms, at least have them looked at by an attorney or business consultant to make sure you're on the right track.

If your entity selection is a corporation, your necessary documents will include articles of incorporation, bylaws and often a shareholders' agreement.

ARTICLES OF INCORPORATION

Articles of incorporation are necessary to register your corporation in your state and it also acts to formally recognize the establishment of your corporation. It will outline the basic information needed to form a corporation, the governance of a corporation, and the relevant and controlling corporate statutes in the state where the articles of incorporation are filed. Some states automatically file them for you when you are incorporating online.

Bylaws

Bylaws are the set of rules and guidelines that your company must follow. They should cover all rules and obligations for shareholders, directors, and officers; the annual meeting rules; the rules on how to remove of officers and directors; stock issuance rules; the corporation's purpose; and the managers and owners' specific duties and obligations.

Under the general definition of bylaws, there are only a few requirements that must be included. At a minimum, you should include the name, purpose, and location of the company's office; the Members of the company; the voting rights and the process by which members are selected; the names of your board of directors; the maximum and minimum amount of directors that are allowed; how to assign new directors; the responsibility of all directors; how long a person can be on the board of directors; the names of all current officers; the process for assigning and removing officers; the duties and responsibilities of officers, members, and directors; when special or annual meetings will take place, the meeting location, and meeting terms; and the rules for amending any current bylaws.

Shareholder Agreement

The shareholder agreement defines the regulations by which your corporation will be run. If you have investors this document establishes how issues are resolved between shareholders as well as defining their individual roles and responsibilities. The article of incorporation serves to identify the individuals in the corporation whereas the shareholder agreement explicitly details their roles and responsibilities. The true purpose of the shareholder agreement is to ensure that all shareholders are treated fairly and that their rights are protected.

If you select to register your business as a limited partnership or limited liability company, the corporate governance documents you need will either be a partnership agreement or operating agreement.

Operating Agreement

An operating agreement should be tailored to your business and not just default to the laws of your company's state of incorporation. It should establish the management structure under which your company operates so there is no room for misinterpretation. At a minimum, your operating agreement should memorialize the company name, address and lawful purpose; your buy-out options; how profits will be allocated; how managers can make decisions and about what; how often managers can be re-elected; contribution deadlines; how and who will perform the accounting of the profits; which accounting method will be used (cash or accrual); define the audit schedule; and how or whether the company can be dissolved by a majority or a unanimous vote.

It is important that you also define each the role of each manager. This gives each manager clear direction and helps manage expectations.

Partnership Agreement

If you have one or more partners, you need a partnership agreement to clearly define the relationship between each partner. At a minimum, a partnership agreement should address decision making, how much each partner is investing as their capital contribution, how much salary each partner is paid, whether they will be repaid for any capital contribution; how much, how frequent and how distributions will be paid; what will happen if one partner dies or becomes incompetent; and what happens when he company needs to be dissolved.

Again, these considerations can get pretty complicated and granular, so if you are not well versed or experienced in this, you really need to get professional advice from an attorney or tax advisor—or both.

COMPLIANCE SNAPSHOT:
WHY YOU NEED CORPORATE
GOVERNANCE DOCUMENTS

You plan to find investors. If you are looking for investors, you need professional and compliant documents to illustrate that you are Potential investors in a business will scrutinize governing documents to understand their rights and obligations should they decide to invest and to determine whether the business has been run in compliance with the documents and applicable law. This is especially true of sophisticated investors such as venture capital and private equity firms, and even "angel" investors. If the documents are considered insufficient and need to be redrafted, this can add substantial expense and delay the closing of a potential equity investment.

You plan to grow and sell. If you plan to sell your business, you need corporate governance documents that clearly define how the merger or sale must be voted on by the owners. If your documents don't include those terms, then you will be held to the rules that are statutory in your state of incorporation, which may or may not be in your favor. Moreover, potential buyers may not be interested in your business if it is not legitimized by having the proper documents.

You plan to have partners. Regardless of who you are going into business with, whether it is your best friend, brother, or a stranger, you need documents that outline each parties' obligations and rights. Do not ever assume that you can work things out over a handshake agreement. Do not let your family make you feel you don't trust them if they are offended that you want to formalize the business relationship. Let them think it is a requirement for investors, merger, or financing because it is. These governing documents define the rights and obligations of the owners on such matters as voting, representation on the board of directors, access to company books and records and the distribution of assets.

CHAPTER 8:

YOUR MISSION STATEMENT

A what? Mission statement? You may be thinking it is not necessary and maybe even slightly stupid. Well, maybe you don't need one, but guess what? It may inspire you to write one. It may inspire others too. And the only reason I care about it is that it is a big draw for investors to know what you stand for.

So, what is a mission statement exactly? Well, you are on a mission, so tell people your "why." It is a heartfelt and emotional plea to your investors and customers, so they know what you're all about.

Technically speaking, it is a simple statement that (somewhat poetically) describes your company's overall purpose and what it contributes to its customers, employees, owners, the planet, and society. You do not have to have all those in your statement, but you choose what imparts your company's "personality" in your words.

Think about your target customer. What would they want to hear? Do they want to hear that you use sustainable packaging? That you donate to charities? That you go the extra mile for safety features? Are ethics, morality, price, or customer service paramount?

Think of it this way: If you were doing a commercial to attract your target customer, what would you say? Depending on your industry, you may want to use hype words or perhaps just have a noticeably clear statement about what your company does without hype words. You may not even want to read this chapter— and hey, that's ok!

First, picture your target customer in your head. What would they want to hear? What would you want to tell them about you, your company and why they should buy from you?

Second, think about what your contribution is to the market and to the world as well as to your customer.

Third, you want to impart why they should buy from your company or why they should buy your product or service. What makes you unique?

Let's look at some large corporate and small startup mission statements for inspiration.

Coca-Cola Company: Refresh the world. Make a difference. Our vision is to craft the brands and choice of drinks that people love, to refresh them in body and spirit. And done in ways that create a more sustainable business and better shared future that makes a difference in people's lives, communities, and our planet[1].

Federal Express: FedEx Corporation will produce superior financial returns for its shareowners by providing high value-added logistics, transportation, and related business services through focused operating companies. Customer requirements

---

[1] https://www.coca-colacompany.com/company/purpose-and-vision

will be met in the highest quality manner appropriate to each market segment served. FedEx will strive to develop mutually rewarding relationships with its team members, partners, and suppliers. Safety will be the first consideration in all operations. Corporate activities will be conducted to the highest ethical and professional standards.[2]

Zenni Optical: To provide the most affordable eyeglasses to people all over the world. To provide the highest-quality **optical** lenses to our customers. To make it easy to order eyeglasses online. To provide exceptional customer support.[3]

Spacemaker: Over the next thirty years, the cities of the world will grow by more than 2 billion people. This makes it necessary to build higher, denser, and faster than before — while also providing high living quality and sustainable urban environments. Achieving this is a global challenge, recognized by the UN's Sustainable Development Goal 11: Sustainable Cities and Communities. The construction industry is struggling to adapt. It is one of the world's largest industries and yet one of the least digitized. Productivity has been falling since the 1950s. Spacemaker is determined to play a vital role in this industry's needed transformation. By dramatically improving decision support and collaboration in real estate development, we aim to help build sustainable and better cities to live in[4].

---

[2] https://investors.fedex.com/company-overview/mission-and-goals/default. aspx

[3] https://www.zennioptical.com/c/about-us

[4] https://www.spacemakerai.com/about/about

Etsy: Our mission is to Keep Commerce Human. People make Etsy possible. We provide a meaningful space for sellers to turn their creative passions into opportunities. We enable buyers to discover unique items made with care. And we treat our employees and our community with respect. We're here because the world needs less of the same and more of the special. Dedication to our mission is at the core of our identity. It guides our day-to-day decisions while inspiring us to think big for the long term. It reflects what makes our marketplace so special and our commitment to having a positive social, economic, and environmental impact.[5]

Personally, I think these mission statements are inspirational and help investors get a feel for who you are and what your company means; if you are trying to sell an idea, the mission statement is the best place to start. People are more likely to invest in a product and purchase a product that gives them an *experience* or a *positive emotional response*. Use the mission statement as an opportunity to give you customers and potential investors all the "feels."

So now you have learned that you have the mindset of an entrepreneur, you have learned the basics about business terms. You have come up with an idea for your business. You have drafted an action plan and business plan, maybe even tackled the business model. You have selected your legal business entity and have incorporated your business. You know how to track your revenue and calculate gross and net profits. You have drafted your Mission Statement and have a clear idea of what kind of entrepreneur you want to be. *Now, how the hell are we gonna pay for all this?* Let's talk about money.

---

[5] https://www.etsy.com/mission

CHAPTER 9:

UNDERSTANDING FUNDING AND CAPITAL

Money. It is kind of the whole point here—you want to make it but first you need to make it?

People are largely creeped out talking about money and have a troubled relationship with money. Money is freedom, freedom is happiness. Therefore, I take the position that money can buy happiness. When you aren't worried about putting food on the table or the power getting shut off, you would be amazed how much money affects our mood. Don't be shy to talk about money and how much you want it.

So how do you fund your brilliant idea? Startup capital. Startup capital is the money you will need to secure so you can get the business going and make your first round of initial costs.

Sometimes people call it seed capital, but that can mean a whole different thing if you are looking for investors and the company needs to look attractive quickly. Start-up capital is just the money you need to get the business going. You may see the two terms used interchangeably, but they can mean something different. More on that later.

Entrepreneurs looking to raise capital will need a solid business plan, a business model and possibly even a prototype of their product to attract financiers, investors, or lenders. There are many sources for money, such as family and friends, venture capitalists, angel investors, and traditional banks. The type of financing you will secure will depend on whether you are going to take your company public or grow a business empire to keep in the family.

Before we get into the diverse types of financing for your startup capital, you need to first estimate how much money you will need. To determine your startup costs, first start with whether you will be brick-and-mortar, solely online, or a service provider, or a combination of those. You may be a service provider with a brick-and-mortar store or an online store with a pop-up shop.

All businesses will likely need a website and marketing. Some businesses will need to purchase inventory, hire service providers, pay salaries, pay for licenses and insurance. You may need assistance from an attorney, accountant, or a consultation with a business professional. You may even just be doing this while you are working full time, and you have a few startup costs and your own labor.

Keep in mind, this exercise contemplates a years' worth of costs. You may only need to have a few months saved, depending on how fast you make a profit. Review the first table below to see a sample of how to calculate your startup capital.

Then use the second table to check off and add your own expenses. There are some blank fields to add in items that are not on the list. This check list will track your monthly recurring expenses, your one-time costs and year one (1) costs.

Sample: Estimated Costs and Recurring Expenses				
A	**B**	**C**	**D**	**E**
ITEM	COST per month	One-time fee	QUANTITY	TOTAL
OFFICE SPACE	$2000 per month		12	$24,000
UTILITIES	$150 per month		12	$1800
OFFICE SUPPLIES	$50 per month		12	$600
ATTORNEY		$4000		$4000
ACCOUNTANT		$2500		$2500
INSURANCE	$200 per month		12	$2400
BUSINESS LICENSE		$395	1	$395
PERMITS	NA			
COMPUTERS		$1000 each	5	$5000
MOBILE PHONES	$500 per month		1 plan 4 phones x 12	$6000
TABLETS	NA			
MARKET RESEARCH		$1000	1	$1000
MARKETING	$2000 per month		12	$24,000
ADVERTISING	$2000 per month		12	$24,000
SALARIES	$30,000 per month		12	$350,0000
NETWORKING GROUPS		$1000	1	$1000
WEBSITE		Build-out $2500	1	$2500
WEBSITE HOSTING	$200 per month		12	$2400
	Recurring Costs by Month	One Time Fees		Total Expenses Year 1
Grand Totals	37, 100	11, 395		$445, 200

Your Estimated Costs and Recurring Expenses

A	B	C	D	E
ITEM		One-time fee	QUANTITY	TOTAL
OFFICE SPACE				
UTILITIES				
OFFICE SUPPLIES				
ATTORNEY				
ACCOUNTANT				
INSURANCE				
BUSINESS LICENSE				
PERMITS				
COMPUTERS				

	Recurring Costs by Month	One Time Fees		Total Expenses Year 1
MOBILE PHONES				
TABLETS				
MARKET RESEARCH				
MARKETING				
ADVERTISING				
SALARIES				
NETWORKING GROUPS				
WEBSITE				
WEBSITE HOSTING				
Grand Totals				

BOOTSTRAPPING

Self-funding is also called bootstrapping. The sources of capital are your own savings, borrowing against your home, borrowing against your 401K, cashing out your 401K, cashing out investments, borrowing from your family and friends.

Bootstrapping gives you complete control of your own company, but before you cash out your investments, be sure to calculate how much money it will cost in penalties and fees to access your retirement or investment accounts.

FACTORING OR MERCHANT CASH ADVANCES

If your products or services will bring in daily "receivables" you can apply for a cash advance. This is an option for businesses with owners that have poor credit but large daily or weekly deposits.

As mentioned earlier, this is called factoring. Factoring can provide a business with almost immediate cash in hand based on the company's based on its future income

Simply put, you are selling a percentage of your future receivables to a financial provider (called a factor) and receiving cash in advance.

CROWDFUNDING

Crowdfunding is getting small amounts of money from many people—those are your crowdfunders. There are online platforms where you can go and pitch your ideas to thousands of investors. The best feature of crowdfunding is that it is low risk, depending on which platform you use.

You will get to retain full control of your idea, which is important to most entrepreneurs. Also, if your business is a flop, you may have no obligation to repay your investors. Again, because each platform is different, make sure you read and understand every single rule and every financial and legal obligation that you are committing yourself too. This is a complicated subject, so I dedicated the entire next chapter to it.

DEBT FINANCING

This is a loan based on your personal credit if your company is new or against your company has established good business credit. Before applying, make sure all business records are complete and organized. You will likely need a business plan as well. You fill out the application, provide the documents, the bank runs your credit and gives you the money.

The bank will then set up your payment plan, very much like a mortgage. Remember, you will be required to keep these monthly payments so factor that into your other monthly business expenses before you decide to take out a big loan. One great advantage to receiving this type of seed capital is that the funds are yours and you do not have an investor telling you how to run your company.

EQUITY FINANCING

A venture capitalist is usually a firm, not a financier. That means you also must deal with teams of lawyers, accountants, investment advisors who perform due diligence on any potential investment, partners, and lots and lots....and lots...of different personalities. Venture capital firms typically finance exceptionally large deals, and the due diligence can be brutal.

MEZZANINE CAPITAL

Mezzanine capital is the love child of debt and equity financing and is meant to be short term financing for businesses with a superior performance history. A mezzanine loan operates like a bridge loan, only you don't need to back it with collateral (that means it is unsecured). The purpose is to provide short-term financing for small business owners and entrepreneurs. They are high-cost loans, but they can help a business get to the next level, such as a public offering.

ANGEL INVESTORS

Angel investors are exactly what they sound like: angels. This type of investor is investing in you and your idea personally—they are venture capitalists who prefer involvement in your idea and often act as an advisor as well. Most often, they are established entrepreneurs who enjoy the thrill of the idea and who often use their profits to get involved in more projects with other entrepreneurs.

HOW IT ALL WORKS TOGETHER

A new company will most likely go through distinct phases of financing unless the company creates a heavy cash flow right out of the gates, which is most likely not going to happen for most entrepreneurs. The order of financing would be seed capital, venture capital, mezzanine funding and then the initial public offering.

Seed capital is usually the smallest amount of financing because it is just meant to cover the initial costs to grow the company in its initial phase. Then, if the company is successful in this first phase, the success can be used to attract venture capitalists.

Venture capitalists, who tend to do a lot of due diligence and consideration before they invest, are likely to invest a lot of money because they have determined that the company should go public and then when the company has its IPO, they have a huge payday.

Because financing is probably the most important part of this process, make sure you have an accountant, financial advisor or attorney weigh in on your decision. Funding and investing have many rules and you do not want to unwittingly break the law and have the Securities Exchange Commission (SEC) chasing you down on fraud charges.

Also, money COSTS money, so be sure you are making a wise choice that will not hurt you later in this process, such as a balloon payment you cannot make or a merchant cash advance that has become too costly. So, at this point, we are established and funded. Now you need to learn about employees. When to hire, when to fire, how to onboard them and terminate them and how to not say the wrong thing while they are under your employ. Let's roll!

CHAPTER 10:

CROWDFUNDING

What is Crowdfunding? Quite literally, it is using a crowd to fund your business.

Crowdfunding is a way of raising capital or funds for a project, venture, or cause by obtaining insignificant amounts of money from a large number of people, typically via the internet. It's essentially a form of crowdsourcing financial support.

Crowdfunding is a broad term that encompasses various methods of raising capital from a large number of individuals, typically through online platforms. Crowdfunding can take different forms, including rewards-based crowdfunding (backers receive a product or service in exchange for their contribution), donation-based crowdfunding (contributors donate without expecting anything in return), and equity-based crowdfunding (investors receive equity in the company in exchange for their investment).

Each type has its own dynamics and legal considerations.

REWARDS BASED CROWDFUNDING
Thanks to social media platforms and the rise of digital marketing, rewards based crowdfunding platforms are sprouting up everywhere. Rewards-based crowdfunding is a super popular capital raining method for entrepreneurs, creators, and

innovators to raise funds for their projects. Unlike traditional fundraising methods that rely on investors or loans, rewards-based crowdfunding involves offering backers tangible rewards or perks in exchange for their contributions. This is such a great option for start-ups.

One of the defining characteristics of rewards-based crowdfunding is the variety of incentives offered to backers, ranging from early access to the product or service being developed to exclusive merchandise, experiences, or acknowledgments. These rewards serve as a way to incentivize potential backers to contribute to the campaign, providing them with a tangible benefit for their support.

For project creators, rewards-based crowdfunding offers a platform to showcase their ideas, products, or services to a wider audience and validate market demand before going into full-scale production. By engaging directly with backers throughout the campaign, creators can gather feedback, refine their offerings, and build a community around their project, laying the groundwork for future success.

The success of a rewards-based crowdfunding campaign often hinges on the effectiveness of the rewards structure and the ability of the project creator to communicate their vision and value proposition to potential backers. Campaigns that offer compelling rewards, set realistic funding goals, and effectively communicate their story and mission are more likely to resonate with backers and achieve their fundraising targets.

Furthermore, rewards-based crowdfunding platforms provide creators with valuable resources and tools to manage their campaigns, including built-in payment processing, marketing features, and analytics dashboards. These platforms serve as a centralized hub for creators to promote their projects, track contributions, and stay connected with their backers, streamlining the fundraising process, and maximizing the chances of success.

Overall, rewards-based crowdfunding has democratized the fundraising landscape, empowering creators to turn their ideas into reality with the support of a global community of backers. By offering a mutually beneficial exchange between creators and backers, rewards-based crowdfunding has revolutionized the way projects are funded, enabling innovation, creativity, and entrepreneurship to flourish in this new and amazing digital age.

HOW TO MARKET CROWDFUNDING PROJECT
Marketing a rewards-based crowdfunding campaign involves several key steps to effectively reach and engage potential backers:

Define your target audience: Understand who your ideal backers are. Consider their demographics, interests, and online behaviors to tailor your marketing efforts effectively.

Create compelling content: Develop engaging content that clearly communicates your project's purpose, value proposition, and the benefits backers will receive. This includes a captivating campaign video, impactful images, and persuasive copywriting.

Choose the right platform: Select a crowdfunding platform that aligns with your project's goals and target audience. Platforms like Kickstarter, Indiegogo, and GoFundMe are popular choices for rewards-based campaigns.

Set realistic funding goals and rewards: Ensure your funding goal is achievable and accurately reflects the costs of your project. Offer enticing rewards at various contribution levels to incentivize backers to support your campaign.

Build anticipation before launch: Generate excitement and anticipation for your campaign by teasing it on social media, email newsletters, and other marketing channels. Share behind-the-scenes content, sneak peeks, and progress updates to engage your audience and build momentum.

Leverage social media: Utilize social media platforms to amplify your campaign's reach and visibility. Share engaging posts, interact with your audience, and encourage supporters to share your campaign with their networks.

Engage with your community: Foster a sense of community and connection with your backers by responding to comments, answering questions, and providing regular updates throughout the campaign.

Reach out to influencers and media: Identify influencers, bloggers, journalists, and industry experts who may be interested in your project and reach out to them with personalized pitches. Securing media coverage and endorsements can significantly boost your campaign's visibility and credibility.

Run targeted advertising campaigns: Invest in targeted advertising campaigns on platforms like Facebook, Instagram, and Google Ads to reach potential backers based on their interests, demographics, and online behavior.

Optimize for search engines: Ensure your campaign page is optimized for search engines by using relevant keywords, descriptive titles, and high-quality imagery. This can help improve your campaign's visibility in search engine results and attract organic traffic.

Offer limited-time incentives and promotions: Create a sense of urgency and encourage immediate action by offering limited-time incentives, early-bird discounts, or exclusive perks for early backers.

Follow up with backers: After the campaign ends, keep your backers informed about your progress, milestones, and any updates related to the project. Show appreciation for their support and continue to nurture your relationship with them beyond the campaign.

DONATION-BASED CROWDFUNDING

Donation-based crowdfunding has emerged as a powerful tool for individuals, organizations, and causes seeking financial support from a broad community of donors. Unlike other forms of crowdfunding where backers expect some form of reward or equity in return for their contribution, donation-based crowdfunding operates on the principle of altruism, with contributors giving without the expectation of receiving anything tangible in return.

One of the key features of donation-based crowdfunding is its ability to mobilize support for a wide range of causes, from personal emergencies and medical expenses to community projects, charitable endeavors, and creative ventures. This inclusive nature enables individuals and groups facing financial challenges to tap into the generosity of a global audience, often reaching far beyond their immediate social circles.

The rise of online crowdfunding platforms has democratized the fundraising process, allowing anyone with internet access to create a campaign and share their story with potential donors worldwide. This accessibility has been particularly beneficial for marginalized communities, grassroots initiatives, and charitable organizations, providing them with a platform to amplify their voices and rally support for their causes.

Moreover, donation-based crowdfunding not only serves as a financial lifeline for those in need but also fosters a sense of connection and solidarity within communities. By allowing individuals to contribute even small amounts, crowdfunding campaigns harness the collective power of micro-donations, demonstrating that every contribution, no matter how modest, can make a meaningful difference in someone's life or in addressing pressing social issues. Truly, donation-based crowdfunding exemplifies the altruistic spirit of humanity, showcasing the capacity for compassion and generosity to effect positive change in the world.

EQUITY CROWDFUNDING (REGULATION CF)

Equity based crowdfunding is highly regulated and not for everyone hence my in-depth description of its mechanics. Regulation Crowdfunding (Reg CF), established under Section 4(a)(6) of the Securities Act of 1933, is a set of rules and regulations implemented by the U.S. Securities and Exchange Commission (SEC) to govern equity crowdfunding. This regulation allows private companies to raise capital from a large number of investors, including non-accredited investors, through various crowdfunding platforms. Regulation Crowdfunding is designed to facilitate capital formation for small businesses and startups while providing some investor protection measures. It truly strikes a balance between enabling access to capital for businesses and safeguarding the interests of investors. It became effective in May 2016, and its rules have since undergone some amendments to refine and improve the regulatory framework.

Key features of Regulation Crowdfunding include:

1. **Limit on Capital Raised:** Companies can raise a maximum aggregate amount of $5 million within a 12-month period through crowdfunding offerings.

2. **Individual Investment Limits:** There are limits on the amount individual investors can contribute. The limits are based on the investor's income and net worth to protect against large financial risks for non-accredited investors.

3. **Intermediary Platforms:** Crowdfunding offerings must be conducted through an SEC-registered intermediary, typically a crowdfunding platform or a broker-dealer.

4. **Disclosure Requirements:** Companies are required to provide certain disclosures to investors, including information about the business, the terms of the offering, the use of funds, and the company's financial condition. These documents should be drafted by an attorney well versed in Crowdfunding.

5. **Financial Statements:** Depending on the amount being raised, companies may need to provide financial statements, which can vary in complexity.

6. **Ongoing Reporting:** Companies that raise funds through Reg CF are subject to ongoing reporting requirements, providing updates to investors and the SEC on their financial condition. A lot of this information will be housed on your investor portal. (More on that below).

Key Terms you need to know:
In a Reg CF offering, there are several key parties involved in the process. These parties play different roles in facilitating and participating in the crowdfunding campaign. Here are the main parties:

1. **Issuer:** The issuer is the company or entity seeking to raise funds through a crowdfunding offering. This could be a startup, small business, or entrepreneur looking for capital to support a specific project or business expansion.

2. **Investors:** Investors are individuals who contribute funds to the crowdfunding campaign. Regulation Crowdfunding allows both accredited and non-accredited investors to participate, subject to certain investment limits based on income and net worth.

3. **Intermediary (Platform):** The crowdfunding platform, also known as an intermediary, is an SEC-registered entity that facilitates the offering. Examples of crowdfunding platforms include websites like Kickstarter, Indiegogo, and others. These platforms connect issuers with potential investors, host the offering details, and manage the transaction process.

4. **SEC (Securities and Exchange Commission):** The SEC is the regulatory body overseeing securities offerings, including Regulation Crowdfunding. Issuers must file the necessary disclosure documents with the SEC, and the SEC reviews and regulates the offerings to ensure compliance with the rules.

5. **Escrow Service:** Funds raised during the crowdfunding campaign are typically held in escrow until a specified funding target is reached. If the target is not met, funds may be returned to investors. Once the target is reached, the funds are released to the issuer.

6. **Legal and Financial Professionals:** Issuers often work with legal and financial professionals to ensure compliance with regulatory requirements, prepare necessary disclosure documents, and provide guidance on financial matters.

7. **Third-Party Service Providers:** Depending on the nature of the offering, issuers may engage third-party service providers for tasks such as marketing, video production, or other specialized services to enhance their crowdfunding campaign. (Click Funnels!)

The Reg CF Process:
Starting a Regulation Crowdfunding (Reg CF) campaign involves several steps, and it's important to navigate the process carefully to comply with SEC regulations. Here is an overview of the key steps to start a Regulation Crowdfunding campaign under Section 4(a)(6):

1. **Eligibility Check:**
   - Ensure that your business is eligible to use Regulation Crowdfunding. This typically applies to U.S.-based companies.
   - Confirm that your fundraising goals align with the maximum limit of $5 million within a 12-month period.

2. **Choose a Crowdfunding Platform:**
   - Select an SEC-registered crowdfunding platform to host your campaign. Make sure the platform complies with the regulatory requirements for intermediaries. I recommend reviewing other companies on a particular platform to find the platform that aligns with your companies' values and image.

3. **Due Diligence:**
   - Conduct due diligence on the crowdfunding platform to understand its terms, fees, and processes.
   - Prepare any required legal and financial documentation, including financial statements and disclosure documents.

4. **File Form C with the SEC:**
   - Prepare and file Form C with the Securities and Exchange Commission (SEC). This form includes essential details about your business, the terms of the offering, and other relevant information.
   - Pay the necessary filing fees.

5. **Approval and Launch:**
   - Wait for the SEC to review and qualify your offering. Once qualified, you can launch your crowdfunding campaign on the chosen platform.

6. **Marketing and Promotion:**
   - Develop a marketing strategy to promote your crowdfunding campaign. Engage with your network, potential investors, and utilize the platform's resources for marketing.

7. **Offering Period:**
   - The crowdfunding campaign will have a set offering period, during which investors can contribute funds. This period typically lasts up to 12 months.

8. **Updates and Communications:**
   - Provide regular updates to investors through the crowdfunding platform. Keep investors informed about the progress of the campaign, use of funds, and other relevant developments.

9. **Escrow and Funding:**
   - Funds raised during the campaign are often held in escrow until the funding target is reached. If the target is met, funds are released to the issuer; otherwise, they may be returned to investors.

10. **Ongoing Reporting:**
    - Comply with ongoing reporting requirements as mandated by the SEC. This includes regular updates on the company's financial condition and other relevant information.

How To Prepare To File For a Regulation Crowdfunding, under Section 4(A)(6):

To file a Regulation Crowdfunding offering under Section 4(a)(6), you'll need to prepare and submit various documents to the U.S. Securities and Exchange Commission (SEC). Here is a general list of documents required:

1. **Form C: Offering Statement:** This is the primary document filed with the SEC. It includes details about the issuer, the offering, and the terms of the securities being offered.

2. **Financial Statements:** Depending on the amount being raised, you may need to provide financial statements. For offerings of $107,000 to $535,000, you need to provide financial statements reviewed by an independent accountant. For offerings over $535,000, audited financial statements are required.

3. **Business Plan:** A detailed business plan outlining the company's operations, management team, products or services, and financial projections.

4. **Use of Proceeds:** An explanation of how the funds raised through the crowdfunding campaign will be used.

5. **Material Risk Factors:** Disclosures about the risks associated with investing in the offering. This is an important section for informing potential investors.

6. **Issuer's Compensation:** Details about any compensation the issuer or its officers and directors expect to receive from the offering.

7. **Offering Price and Method:** Information about the offering price and how it was determined.

8. **Target Offering Amount and Deadline:** The target amount of funds the issuer is seeking to raise and the deadline for reaching that amount.

9. **Ownership and Capitalization Table:** Details about the current ownership structure of the company and how it will change after the offering.

10. **Disclosure of Related Party Transactions:** Any transactions between the issuer and its officers, directors, or significant shareholders.

11. **Background of the Issuer and Management Team:** Information about the background and experience of the issuer and its key management personnel.

These are general requirements, and specific details may vary based on your unique situation. It's crucial to thoroughly review the SEC's instructions and regulations related to Regulation Crowdfunding and seek legal advice to ensure compliance.

Marketing and advertising a Regulation Crowdfunding (Reg CF) campaign under Section 4(a)(6) involves promoting your offering to potential investors while adhering to SEC regulations.

Before Form C is filed, Issuers are allowed to promote and advertise in order to "feel out" public interest. This is called "Testing the waters" and it refers to the ability of issuers to gauge investor interest before officially filing Form C with the Securities and Exchange Commission (SEC) for a Regulation Crowdfunding (Reg CF) offering under Section 4(a)(6). There are two phases to consider: pre-filing "testing the waters" and post-filing with limits on advertising.

1. **Testing the Waters (Pre-filing):**
   - Before filing Form C, issuers are allowed to engage in activities to test investor interest. This can include discussions with potential investors, providing them with information about the planned offering, and seeking indications of interest.
   - During this phase, issuers are not required to use a specific platform or intermediary. They can use various means, such as social media, email, or in-person meetings, to communicate with potential investors.
   - Importantly, any materials shared during this phase must not constitute an offer to sell securities. The purpose is to assess investor interest without making formal investment offers.

2. **Permitted with Limits on Advertising (Post-filing):**
   - After filing Form C with the SEC, issuers can continue to advertise the offering but with certain limitations. The advertising must be done through the registered crowdfunding platform chosen by the issuer.
   - Advertising is restricted to the communication channels provided by the platform. The intermediary (platform) is responsible for ensuring that the advertising materials comply with SEC regulations and do not contain misleading information.
   - Issuers are not allowed to make offers outside of the platform, and all investment transactions must occur through the registered intermediary.

It is recommended to have a compliance attorney who specializes in Social Media Marketing review your advertisements and social media posts to ensure compliance with all regulations, including those that fall under specific industries as well as the Federal Trade commission (FTC).

3. **Offering Conducted on an Internet Platform through a Registered Intermediary:**
   - The actual offering, including the acceptance of investments, must take place on an SEC-registered crowdfunding platform.
   - The intermediary on the platform facilitates the transactions, ensures compliance with regulations, and provides a secure environment for investors to participate.

Effectively Marketing Your Reg CF:
Here are some steps to effectively market and advertise your Reg CF campaign:

1. **Create a Compelling Story:**
   - Craft a compelling and transparent narrative about your company. Clearly communicate your mission, product, or service, and why investors should be excited about supporting your venture.

2. **Build a Professional Campaign Page:**
   - Use a reputable crowdfunding platform to host your campaign. Design a professional-looking campaign page with engaging visuals, videos, and a detailed description of your business.

3. **Utilize Social Media:**
   - Leverage social media platforms to create awareness about your campaign. Share updates, behind-the-scenes content, and milestones. Engage with your audience and encourage them to share your campaign.

4. **Email Marketing:**
   - Build an email list of potential investors and regularly update them about your campaign progress. Consider creating a newsletter to keep supporters informed and engaged.

5. **Public Relations (PR):**
   - Reach out to relevant media outlets and industry publications to get coverage for your campaign. A well-placed article or interview can significantly boost visibility.

6. **Educational Content:**
   - Create content that educates potential investors about crowdfunding, your industry, and the specific benefits of investing in your company. Blog posts, webinars, and infographics can be effective.

7. **Engage with Your Network:**
   - Tap into your existing network of friends, family, colleagues, and industry connections. Host a ZOOM call or party to "launch" your product. Personal recommendations and word-of-mouth can be powerful.

8. **Influencer Marketing:**
   - Identify influencers or thought leaders in your industry who may be interested in supporting or endorsing your campaign. Their endorsement can lend credibility to your offering. This is a great opportunity for affiliate marketing using social media influencers.

9. **Community Engagement:**
   - Participate in relevant forums, online communities, and events related to your industry. Engage with potential investors and answer their questions.

10. **Compliance with SEC Regulations:**
    - Ensure that all marketing materials, including online and offline content, comply with SEC regulations. Avoid making exaggerated claims or promises and provide clear and accurate information. Have a Social Media Compliance attorney review your copy to create a compliance trail. Any claims made need to be backed up and substantiated with documentary evidence. Create a drive to house this data.

11. **Targeted Advertising:**
    - Use targeted online advertising to reach potential investors. Platforms like social media and Google Ads allow you to tailor your ads to specific demographics.

12. **Offline Events:**
    - Consider hosting or participating in offline events, such as industry conferences or local meetups, to connect with potential investors in person.

Always prioritize transparency and compliance with SEC rules to build trust with investors. Consult legal professionals experienced in securities laws to review your marketing materials and ensure they meet regulatory requirements.

OTHER ELEMENTS TO CONSIDER:

Market Reach: Determine your social media reach and engagement. This can be done by a social media company to determine your engagement.

Define Goals for the Raise: Define amount of capital to be raised. Create a budget, a timeline, and a pitch for campaign.

1. **Create Awards and Offers:** Rewards are incentives that you offer to your backers in exchange for their pledges. They can be physical products, digital downloads, experiences, recognition, or anything else that is relevant and valuable to your project and your audience. Rewards should be creative, appealing, and feasible. You need to consider the costs, the delivery, and the fulfillment of your rewards. You also need to create different tiers of rewards for different levels of pledges.

2. **Effective Promotions:** Click funnel will be created to launch. Promote your campaign to your existing network and grow your network and engagement with specific social media campaigns. You can use social media, email, blogs, podcasts, press releases, events, and word-of-mouth to spread the word. You need to have a marketing strategy that identifies your target audience, your message, your channels, and your timeline. You also need to engage with your audience, answer their questions, and update them on your progress.

3. **Delivery of Awards and Offers:** You need to thank your backers, update them on your project status, and fulfill your rewards. You also need to report on how you used the funds, what challenges you faced, and what outcomes you achieved. You need to be transparent, accountable, and respectful. This will help you build trust, loyalty, and reputation for your project and yourself.

TOOLS FOR EFFECTIVE CROWDFUNDING MARKETING CAMPAIGNS

1. **KEYWORD RESEARCH TOOLS:** Keyword research is the process of finding and analyzing the words and phrases that your potential readers use to search for information online. Keyword research tools help you discover what topics are popular, relevant, and profitable for your niche. They also help you optimize your content for search engines and rank higher on the results pages. Google Keyword Planner, Ubersuggest, and SEMrush.

2. **Content Creation Tools:** Content creation is the process of producing and editing your blog posts, images, videos, podcasts, or other types of content. Content creation tools help you generate ideas, write better headlines, format your text, check your grammar, design your visuals, and more. They can improve your content quality, readability, and appeal. CoSchedule Headline Analyzer, Grammarly, and Canva.

3. **Content Distribution Tools:** Content distribution is the process of sharing and promoting your content across different channels and platforms. Content distribution tools help you automate, schedule, and track your content

performance on social media, email, or other networks. They can increase your content reach, engagement, and traffic.Buffer, Mailchimp, and Medium.

4. **Content Analytics Tools:** Content analytics tools help you collect, visualize, and interpret data on your content metrics, such as views, clicks, shares, comments, conversions, and more. They can help you evaluate your content effectiveness, identify your strengths and weaknesses, and optimize your content strategy. Google Analytics, BuzzSumo, and HubSpot.

5. **Content Management Tools:** Content management is the process of organizing and maintaining your content assets and resources. Content management tools help you store, access, update, and manage your content in a centralized and secure place. They can help you streamline your content workflow, collaborate with your team, and ensure consistency and quality. Some of the most effective content management tools are WordPress, Dropbox, and Trello.

6. **Content Learning Tools:** Content learning is the process of acquiring and updating your content knowledge and skills. Content learning tools help you access, consume, and apply the latest trends, insights, and best practices in content marketing. They can help you improve your content expertise, creativity, and innovation. Some of the most effective content learning tools are Content Marketing Institute, Udemy, and Skillshare.

PROMOTING THROUGH CLICK FUNNELS:

A click funnel, often referred to as a sales funnel or marketing funnel, is a visual representation of the stages that a potential customer goes through before making a purchase or taking a desired action. The term "click funnel" emphasizes the online nature of these processes, where user interactions are often initiated by clicking on links, buttons, or advertisements.

The most common stages of a click funnel include:

1. **Awareness:** At the top of the funnel, individuals become aware of a product, service, or brand. This can happen through various channels such as social media, search engines, or online advertising.

2. **Interest:** In this stage, potential customers express interest in the offering. They may click on an ad, visit a website, or sign up for newsletters to learn more.

3. **Consideration:** At this point, individuals are actively considering the product or service. They may engage with content, compare options, and seek more detailed information.

4. **Intent:** Users in this stage have demonstrated a strong interest and are showing signs of intent to make a purchase. They may have added items to a shopping cart or initiated the checkout process.

5. **Desired Action:** The final stage involves the actual conversion, where the individual becomes a customer by completing a purchase or taking the desired action.

With a Reg CF, the desired action is the potential investor creating a profile in your portal.

6. **Post-Conversion Engagement**: After the potential investor completes the investor information form, there may be additional stages for post-conversion engagement, such as providing feedback, requesting support, or joining loyalty programs.

A click funnel is often visualized as a series of interconnected pages or steps, with each step designed to guide the user through the conversion process. Online tools and platforms, like ClickFunnels, help businesses create and optimize these funnels, allowing for the seamless movement of users from one stage to the next.

The goal of a click funnel is to streamline the user journey, provide relevant information at each stage, and increase the likelihood of conversion. It's a fundamental concept in digital marketing and e-commerce, helping businesses map out and optimize the customer acquisition process.

Here is a checklist to track your Regulation Crowdfunding Journey!

PRE-FILING		
Date Started:	Task:	Date Completed:
	Understand Reg CF Requirements: Familiarize yourself with the SEC regulations governing Reg CF offerings.	

	Determine Eligibility: Confirm that your company meets the eligibility criteria for a Reg CF offering.	
	Select a Crowdfunding Platform: Choose a registered crowdfunding platform to host your campaign.	
	Legal Counsel: Consult with legal professionals experienced in securities laws to guide you through the process.	
	Business Plan: Develop a comprehensive business plan that outlines your company's mission, products/services, and financial projections.	
	Financial Statements: Prepare the necessary financial statements based on the offering amount (reviewed or audited, as required).	
	Offering Terms: Determine the terms of your offering, including the target amount, offering price, and use of proceeds.	

	Marketing Materials: Create engaging and compliant marketing materials, including a campaign page, videos, and visuals.	
	(Pre-Filing)Testing the Waters: Engage in Preliminary Discussions. If desired, engage in discussions with potential investors to gauge interest before filing Form C.	
	Complete Form C: Prepare and file Form C with the SEC, providing all required information about your offering.	
POST FILING		
	Legal Review: Have legal professionals review your Form C to ensure compliance with SEC regulations.	
	(Post-Filing) Advertise on Platform: Advertise your offering within the limits allowed by the platform after Form C is filed.	

	Engage with Investors: Use social media, email, and other channels to engage with potential investors within the platform's guidelines.	
	(Post-Filing) Respond to Investor Questions: Be responsive to inquiries from potential investors and provide transparent and accurate information.	
	Monitor Campaign Progress: Regularly monitor the progress of your campaign and make adjustments as needed.	
CLOSING THE OFFERING		
	Complete Offering: Once the target amount is reached, follow the platform's procedures to close the offering.	
	File Form C-U: File Form C-U with the SEC to report the final results of the offering.	
	Communicate with Investors: Communicate with investors about the closing of the offering and any relevant updates.	

Notes and/or Questions:

PRE-FILING QUESTIONNAIRE

Issuer Information:

1. **Company Name:**
   - Provide the legal name of your company.

2. **Entity Type:**
   - Specify the legal structure of your company (e.g., corporation, LLC).

3. **Date of Incorporation:**
   - Provide the date when your company was incorporated.

4. **Business Address:**
   - Share the physical location of your business.

Reg CF Eligibility:

5. **Annual Revenue:**
   - What is your company's annual revenue for the most recent fiscal year?

6. **Offering Amount:**
   - Indicate the amount you intend to raise through the Reg CF offering.

7. **Use of Proceeds:**
   - Describe how you plan to use the funds raised through the crowdfunding campaign.

Crowdfunding Platform:

8. **Selected Crowdfunding Platform:**
   - Have you chosen a registered crowdfunding platform for hosting your campaign?

9. **Platform Requirements:**
   - Confirm that you understand and can comply with any specific requirements of the chosen platform.

Legal Compliance:

10. **Legal Counsel:**
    - Have you consulted with legal professionals experienced in securities laws regarding your Reg CF offering?

11. **Testing the Waters:**
    - Did you engage in any activities to test the waters before filing Form C?

12. **Form C Preparation:**
    - Has Form C been prepared with all necessary details about your offering?

13. **Marketing Materials:**
    - Have you created compliant marketing materials for your Reg CF campaign?

Financial Information:

14. **Financial Statements:**
    - Have you prepared the required financial statements (reviewed or audited, as necessary)?

15. Offering Terms:

- What are the specific terms of your offering, including the target amount, offering price, and any other relevant terms?

Advertising and Engagement:

16. Post-Filing Marketing:

- Are you aware of the limitations of advertising after filing Form C?

17. Engagement Strategy:

- How do you plan to engage with potential investors during the campaign?

Timeline:

18. Filing Timeline:

- What is your proposed timeline for filing Form C and launching the crowdfunding campaign?

19. Offering Duration:

- How long do you intend to keep the offering open?

Closing the Offering:

20. Closing Procedures:

- Do you have a plan for closing the offering, including filing Form C-U with the SEC?

21. Communication with Investors:

- How do you plan to communicate with investors post-offering?

This questionnaire is designed to gather essential information from the client and ensure that the attorney has a comprehensive understanding of the client's situation and intentions related to the Regulation Crowdfunding offering. This does not constitute legal advice and is for informational purposes only.

"Disclaimer: The information provided in this document is for general informational purposes only and is not intended as legal advice. It is not a substitute for professional legal counsel tailored to your specific situation. Always consult with a qualified attorney to obtain advice related to your individual circumstances and legal needs."

CHAPTER 11:

THE PITCH DECK

Your pitch deck is like a first date to a potential investor. You must be exciting and alluring, but not too overpowering. You must impart your core values and morals without being a total bore. You want to appear passionate, but not wanton. You must strike it exactly right, or no second date.

So, what exactly is a pitch deck? It is a very concise presentation that outlines the key aspects of your tech start up business, its value proposition, market opportunity, product or service offering, team, and financial projections. The purpose of a pitch deck is to effectively communicate the startup's story and potential to investors, stakeholders, and potential partners. I almost fell asleep writing that—and that is exactly my point! It can be a very dry process, and it needs your personality—your why and your passion—so it will get the right message across. Your pitch deck must also be very visually compelling, so present your data in an easy-to-read format such as line graphs, pie charts, comparison charts, and any other applicable data visualization.

That sounds easy right? Well, that part really is. But getting all the data for all those pretty graphs and charts is not. Make sure you have completed all the necessary steps in the previous chapter, so you have something to present!

Before you start your pitch deck make sure you have all your data, an eye-catching logo, and an amazing photograph of yourself too. If you do not have PowerPoint or you are creatively challenged, there are many applications and software programs with templates you can modify, so you do not need to start from scratch or be stymied from a lack of artistic genius.

Here is a very basic structure for your pitch deck. There is no expected format or formula, so you should tailor it to what you need for your industry.

BASIC PITCH DECK

1. **Cover Slide:**
   Company name/logo
   Tagline or a brief statement that encapsulates the company's mission.

2. **Problem Statement:**
   Clearly define the problem or pain point that the startup aims to address.
   Provide data or statistics to support the significance of the problem.

3. **Solution:**
   Present the startup's unique solution or product offering.
   Explain how the solution solves the identified problem.
   Highlight any competitive advantages or unique selling points.

4. **Market Opportunity:**
   Provide an overview of the target market and its size.
   Showcase market growth trends, potential customer base, and addressable market segments.
   Highlight any barriers to entry or competitive landscape insights.

5. **Product/Service Overview:**
   Provide a high-level overview of the startup's product or service.
   Include visuals, screenshots, or product demonstrations to illustrate the offering.
   Highlight key features and functionalities that differentiate the product in the market.

6. **Business Model:**
   Explain the revenue model and how the startup plans to generate income.
   Discuss pricing strategy, customer acquisition channels, and potential partnerships.
   Present any recurring revenue streams or future monetization opportunities.

7. **Traction and Milestones:**
   Share key achievements and milestones reached to date.
   Highlight any customer acquisition, partnerships, or revenue generation successes.
   Include data on user growth, engagement metrics, or customer testimonials if available.

8. **Market Strategy:**

   Describe the go-to-market strategy for acquiring and retaining customers. Outline the marketing and sales approach, including channels, target audience, and distribution strategy. Discuss any strategic partnerships or collaborations that can enhance market reach.

9. **Team:**

   Introduce the founding team and key members, emphasizing relevant experience and expertise.

   Showcase advisors or industry experts who support the startup.

   Highlight any notable achievements or credentials that validate the team's capabilities.

10. **Financial Projections:**

    Provide a summary of the startup's financial projections, including revenue forecasts, cost structure, and growth metrics.

    Present key financial indicators such as gross margin, customer acquisition costs, and projected profitability.

    Include any funding requirements or use of funds if seeking investment.

11. **Investment Opportunity:**

    Clearly state the amount of investment sought and the equity or stake offered in return.

    Discuss the potential return on investment and exit strategy for investors.

    Summarize the funding timeline and how the investment will be utilized to drive growth.

12. Contact Information:
> Include contact details for the startup, including website, email, and social media handles.
> Encourage interested parties to reach out for more information or to schedule further discussions.

Unless you want people drifting off, checking Instagram, or ordering lunch on their phone, you must present a concise, engaging, and visually appealing pitch deck. Be engaging!

How do you do that? Well, people love graphics and imagery.

Not to get too much off topic, but studies have shown that the human brain makes unique activity patterns with assorted colors and that people are more likely to remember images that are colorful. Color affects people's heart rate and blood pressure.

Choose graphics that are in concert with how you want to make the potential investors feel. You can use graphics that speak to the problem your app solves or the people who will benefit from it. You can choose graphics and colors that are energizing or calming. It depends on your overall "why" and the corporate personality of your company.

You should also use simple, straightforward, and clear language. Limit the use of text on slides, and leverage your graphics, charts, and images to support your company's key messages. Nothing says "invest now" like a fat green histogram with black numbers.

And although people love graphics and imagery, they also relate to people that are engaging, so be funny, smart, warm, and likable.

Now let's pivot to a new thought: you MUST think of your pitch deck as a pretty cue card. It is up to you to fill in all the personality when you deliver your presentation to a group. Never forget that your pitch deck is a deck for your pitch. The pitch is the star of the show because it comes from you, and the deck should act merely as a visual aid to support your narrative during your presentation.

Making a successful pitch to investors is crucial for entrepreneurs seeking funding for their startup. Here are some key strategies to consider:

1. **Know Your Audience**: Research and understand the target investors before the pitch. Learn about their investment preferences, previous investments, and areas of expertise. Tailor your pitch to align with their interests and showcase how your startup fits into their investment thesis.

2. **Develop a Compelling Story:** Craft a compelling narrative that communicates your startup's mission, vision, and the problem it solves. Emphasize the market opportunity and the unique value proposition of your product or service. Engage the investors by sharing personal anecdotes or stories that demonstrate your passion and commitment.

3. **Keep It Concise**: Respect the investors' time and deliver a concise and focused pitch. Aim for a 10-15 minute presentation that covers the key aspects of your business. Capture their attention from the beginning and maintain their interest throughout the pitch.

4. **Clearly Define the Problem and Solution:** Articulate the problem you are addressing and explain how your

116

solution effectively solves it. Use data, examples, and real-life scenarios to illustrate the significance of the problem and the impact of your solution. Be specific about the value proposition and the benefits your product or service offers.

5. **Demonstrate Traction and Proof of Concept**: Provide evidence of market traction and validation. Highlight key milestones, customer acquisition numbers, revenue growth, partnerships, or any relevant traction achieved. This helps build credibility and shows that your startup is gaining market acceptance.

6. **Showcase a Strong Team:** Investors not only invest in ideas but also in the people behind them. Present your team's expertise, relevant industry experience, and accomplishments. Highlight complementary skill sets and demonstrate the team's ability to execute the business plan effectively.

7. **Present a Realistic and Scalable Business Model**: Clearly outline your business model and revenue streams. Showcase how you plan to monetize your product or service and your strategy for achieving profitability. Discuss the scalability of your business, market expansion opportunities, and potential for future revenue growth.

8. **Address Potential Risks and Mitigation Strategies:** Acknowledge and address potential risks and challenges associated with your business. Demonstrate that you have identified these risks and have mitigation strategies in place. This shows investors that you have a realistic

understanding of the market and are prepared to navigate potential obstacles.

9. **Provide a Clear Financial Plan:** Present a detailed financial plan that includes revenue projections, cost structure, and key financial metrics. Discuss your assumptions, market size, and potential return on investment. Be prepared to answer questions about your financial projections and demonstrate a clear understanding of your numbers.

10. **Practice and Seek Feedback:** Practice your pitch repeatedly to refine your delivery and ensure a smooth presentation. Seek feedback from trusted advisors, business coaches, or other entrepreneurs who have successfully pitched to investors before. Incorporate their suggestions and continually iterate to improve your pitch.

11. **Be Authentic and Engage in Dialogue:** Be authentic and passionate during your pitch. Engage in a conversation with the investors, inviting questions and feedback. Listen attentively and respond thoughtfully to their queries. This demonstrates your openness to collaboration and your ability to adapt and learn.

Remember, each pitch is an opportunity to build relationships with investors, so be professional, confident, and receptive to feedback. Do not let your ego stop you from learning how to improve your company, your presentation, or your pitch deck from criticism and feedback. Even if you don't secure funding immediately, a well-executed pitch can leave a positive impression that may lead to future opportunities, aka second dates.

PART THREE:

LAUNCH!

CHAPTER 12:

BUILDING A TEAM

If you are going to scale a business, you need to hire people. The RIGHT people. And then you need to create an environment where your employees feel valued, respected, and happy. This is precisely why hiring the right employees is not just crucial for the success and growth of any business, but for its continued growth and lifetime value. It's a process that requires careful planning, consideration, and a clear understanding of the organization's needs and values.

My philosophy is people will stay if they have one at least one out of three things: respect, money, or freedom. For example. A remote employee may not have the best salary or contact with the office personnel, but the freedom is worth it. Another employee may be making a large salary that is helping them achieve a personal goal and financial freedom, so they can tolerate the lack of recognition. Another employee may be working on a passion project or in a startup and the personal growth and peer recognition make it worth it.

You become a training breeding ground if you do not offer any of those elements to an employee. People will get experience and leave, and employee attrition is costly.

Primarily, businesses should begin by defining the role they seek to fill. This involves creating a detailed job description that outlines the responsibilities, qualifications, and expectations for the position. A well-defined job description not only attracts suitable candidates but also provides a clear benchmark for evaluating applicants. There so many of considerations for this, and it will also help you correctly classify employees as hourly, salary or as independent contractors.

Next, it's important for businesses to consider their company culture and values. A candidate who aligns with the organization's core principles is more likely to thrive in the workplace and contribute positively to the team. During the interview process, assess not only the candidate's skills and experience, but also their cultural fit within the company. I cannot impress the importance of this above everything else; companies that hire talent at lower salaries become breading grounds for someone else's great employee.

Utilizing a multi-channel recruitment strategy is essential and provides a nice way to create a balanced and diverse work environment. This includes posting job openings on various platforms such as company websites, social media, and specialized job boards. Additionally, networking events, industry conferences, and employee referrals can be invaluable sources for identifying potential hires.

The screening process should be thorough and systematic. This can involve reviewing resumes, conducting phone interviews, and administering skills assessments or tests relevant to the position. Each stage of the screening process should be designed to filter out candidates who do not meet the specific requirements outlined in the job description.

Conducting effective interviews is a critical aspect of the hiring process. Interviewers should be prepared with a set of standardized questions that assess both technical competencies and behavioral traits. Behavioral interviews, which focus on past experiences and actions, can provide valuable insights into how a candidate might perform in real-world scenarios.

While evaluating candidates, it's important to consider not only their technical skills, but also their soft skills. These include communication abilities, teamwork, adaptability, and problem-solving capabilities. Soft skills are often equally as important as technical proficiency, particularly in collaborative work environments. You can always teach people how to do something, but you cannot teach someone to be nice!

Reference checks are an essential step in the hiring process. Contacting previous employers or professional references can provide valuable insights into a candidate's work ethic, reliability, and interpersonal skills. This step helps verify the accuracy of information provided by the candidate and can uncover any potential red flags.

Transparency and clear communication are crucial throughout the hiring process. Candidates should be provided with accurate information about the position, company, and expectations. Additionally, businesses should keep candidates informed about the progress of their application and provide timely feedback.

Once a candidate is selected, it's important to extend a job offer promptly. This offer should include details about compensation, benefits, and any other pertinent terms of employment. Businesses should be prepared to negotiate and address any questions or concerns the candidate may have.

Finally, onboarding is a crucial step that sets the tone for a new employee's experience within the company. A comprehensive orientation program should provide the necessary training, resources, and introductions to ensure a smooth transition into the role.

Most people spend more time at work than they do with their families and friends, and this is why hiring employees is a strategic process that requires careful planning, assessment, and consideration. By defining the role, assessing cultural fit, utilizing a multi-channel recruitment strategy, conducting thorough interviews, evaluating both technical and soft skills, conducting reference checks, maintaining transparency, extending offers promptly, and providing a comprehensive onboarding process, businesses can effectively identify and hire the right candidates to contribute to their success and growth. Remember, the investment in a thorough hiring process pays off in the form of a motivated, skilled, and committed workforce.

Once you have your workforce hired and ready, you must keep them happy! Yes, happy!

Creating that happy, positive, and productive work culture is crucial for the success and longevity of any business. A healthy work environment not only fosters employee satisfaction and retention but also enhances creativity, innovation, and overall performance. Before you even hire your first employee, take the time to write out your thoughts on the type of employer you want to be, and what kind of environment you want to create.

Start by identifying and clearly articulating the core values that will guide your business. These values should reflect your company's mission, vision, and long-term goals. Make sure they resonate with employees and serve as a compass for decision-making. You can use the list below as a guide to make your own.

1. **Lead by Example:** The leadership team must embody the values and behaviors you want to instill in the organization. Leaders should set the standard for integrity, accountability, and respect. Their actions and decisions should align with the company's stated values.

2. **Communicate Openly and Transparently:** Establish clear channels of communication that encourage transparency and open dialogue. This includes regular team meetings, one-on-one check-ins, and platforms for anonymous feedback. Transparent communication builds trust and empowers employees to share their ideas and concerns.

3. **Empower and Trust Your Employees:** Provide employees with the autonomy and responsibility to make decisions within their roles. Trusting your team fosters a sense of ownership and accountability, which leads to increased motivation and productivity. Do not micromanage or enforce petty rules that make your company feel like a prison. People have lives and if they are productive, do not be afraid to be flexible when they need it. This fosters goodwill and employees who feel valued do not burn out and leave.

4. **Invest in Employee Development:** Support continuous learning and skill development. Offer training programs, business coach or mentorship opportunities, and resources for personal and professional growth. When employees feel that their development is valued, they are more likely to invest in the success of the business.

5. **Foster Collaboration and Teamwork:** Create an environment where employees are encouraged to collaborate across departments and share knowledge. Foster a sense of camaraderie through team-building activities and projects that require cross-functional cooperation.

6. **Recognize and Reward Achievements:** Acknowledge and celebrate the accomplishments of your employees. Recognition can come in various forms, such as praise, bonuses, promotions, or other incentives. This not only boosts morale but also reinforces positive behaviors.

7. **Promote Work-Life Balance:** Encourage a healthy work-life balance by offering flexible work arrangements, paid time off, and wellness programs. Supporting employees in their personal lives leads to increased satisfaction and productivity in their professional roles.

8. **Prioritize Diversity and Inclusion:** Embrace diversity in all its forms within your workforce. Foster an inclusive environment where all employees feel valued and heard. Actively seek out different perspectives and ensure that your hiring practices promote a diverse team.

9. **Provide a Safe and Supportive Environment:** Ensure that physical and emotional well-being are prioritized. Create a safe and inclusive workplace where employees feel comfortable expressing themselves and seeking help if needed.

10. **Maintain a Results-Oriented Focus:** Emphasize the importance of results and performance over long hours or "busy work." Encourage employees to set clear goals and provide the necessary resources and support for them to achieve those goals.

11. **Adapt and Evolve:** A good culture isn't static; it evolves with the business and its employees. Regularly assess and adapt your practices based on feedback, industry changes, and the evolving needs and expectations of your team.

Creating a solid and balanced culture for your business is a multifaceted endeavor that requires commitment, consistency, and genuine care for your employees. By aligning your values, investing in your team's development, and fostering a positive work environment, you'll lay the foundation for a thriving and successful business. Remember, a healthy culture is not only a benefit to your employees, but also a key driver of your business's long-term success. Turnover is expensive!

CHAPTER 13:

EMPLOYEES AND HUMAN RESOURCE MANAGEMENT

I f you are going to be hiring employees, there are some key functions you need to understand completely to be compliant with your state and federal employment laws. You will not need a full on human resource manager or department unless you plan to hire a lot of people, but keep in mind having a structure in place for the first employee helps you as you add people and grow your business. None of this is legal advice, just some information I gathered and learned over the years, but you should hire a human resource professional once you start adding employees. And always seek the advice of an attorney for employment laws and compliance.

The extremely basic functions of human resource management are recruiting and hiring; maintaining employer-employee relations; facilitating benefits and compensation for the employee on behalf of the employer; ensuring labor compliance on behalf of the employer and training and development.

You should have basic personnel documents prepared when you start hiring. You will need an employee handbook with the rules and expectations of your company, an offer letter template, hiring documents for taxes and payroll, documents for eligibility to work in the United States, documents for writing up employees, and termination documents. Each employee should have their own folder with their hire date on the folder and all their documents contained within the folder.

RECRUITING, HIRING AND FIRING

If you are at the point that you need to hire employees, make a list of the job duties that each job will be performing. This is your framework of the job description. This is important because some employees are legally required to be paid overtime and others are not. Employees will either have exempt and nonexempt status as far as overtime. You will need to decide if you are hiring an hourly or salaried employee before you advertise the position.

SALARY OR HOURLY EMPLOYEES

Try to familiarize yourself with the Fair Labor Standards Act (FLSA). The FLSA is the act that established minimum wage, overtime pay, recordkeeping, and youth employment standards affecting employees in the private sector and in federal, state, and local governments.

Earlier in this chapter we discussed drafting job descriptions and determining what kind of employee you need to hire. This is something you should absolutely consult with an attorney or human resource management professional about before you hire.

So, you can have a salaried employee who is entitled to overtime pay; you can have a salaried employee that is not entitled to overtime pay and then you have hourly employees who must receive overtime pay. This all depends on what job they are doing; what their job duties are and what industry they are working in. Exempt employees are those that are excluded from the overtime pay requirements of the FLSA. These are highly compensated employees, professionals, executives, and information technology professionals. This is not an exhaustive list; but those are the main categories.

Exempt employees are paid a salary and are expected to work beyond their normal work hours for the same pay every pay period without any overtime pay. Non-exempt employees are those eligible for overtime pay of 1.5 times the regular hourly rate of pay for all hours worked over 40 per work week. Let your employees know, in writing, that all overtime must be approved in advance. If you don't, they may work at home and attempt to get paid overtime for work done out of your line of sight.

When you advertise for an employee, those functions and the job description will be used to attract the right people to apply for that position. There are certain items that should not be included in the job description or advertisement and those are all the same items that you are not allowed to ask for during the interview.

WHAT YOU CAN AND CANNOT ASK AN EMPLOYEE CANDIDATE

Illegal job interview questions solicit information from job candidates that could be used to discriminate against them. Asking questions on these topics can result in what is called "charges of discrimination," which is an official investigation by the U.S. Equal Employment Opportunity Commission (EEOC), and potentially a lawsuit can be filed if the issue cannot be resolved by the EEOC. The EEOC will give the candidate what is called a "right to sue," and then a lawsuit can be filed against your company.

The subjects that are off limits are race, color, or national origin; religion; sex, gender identity or sexual orientation; pregnancy status; disability; age or genetic information; citizenship (think of DACA); marital status; family status; and number of children.

APPLICATION AND INTERVIEW QUESTION DOS AND DON'TS

1. Place of Abode
   What you can ask: *Please list your address for the preceding ten years and the length of time at each address.*

   What you may not ask: Do you rent or own your home? With whom do you reside? Are you related to the people that you live with?

2. Age
   What you can ask: *You need not even ask for someone's age as it will be on their government issued identification, which will be needed to prove the right to work. However, you can just ask their age in a straightforward manner, such as "What is your date of birth?" Especially if you are selling products that require the employee to be over eighteen or over twenty-one, such as alcohol, cigarettes, or fireworks.*

   What you may not ask: When did you graduate from high school? What year did you graduate from college?

3. Work Schedule and Availability

   What you can ask: *What days and shifts can you work? Are there shifts you cannot work? Are there any responsibilities you have that could make it difficult for you to travel to work? Do you have a reliable way of getting to work?*

What you may not ask: Are you able to work on Saturdays? This could be construed as trying to ask about religious observance. Are you able to work on Sundays? This could be construed as trying to ask about religious observance. Who watches your children when you are working? What happens if the children are too sick to go to school, who will watch them then? Do you own your own car?

Asking women about childcare is discriminatory. Asking people if they own a car may have a disparate impact on some racial groups, so the EEOC recommends asking as stated above. If the potential hire needs a car for work, then you ask if they have access to a car.

4. Citizenship and National Origin
   Of course, you will need to verify if your potential hire is eligible to work in the United States. How you ask is what counts.

   What you can ask: *Are you legally eligible to work in the United States? Can you show proof of citizenship/visa/ alien registration if we decide to hire you? Are you known by any other names? Can you speak, read, and write English? Do you speak any other languages? (If needed for the position, such as a translator, attorney or community job that necessitates language proficiency).*

   What you may not ask: Can I see your birth certificate? Where were your parents born? Where were you born?

What is your ethnic background? Where did you learn to speak Russian? Are you a U.S. Citizen?

5. Education
What you can ask: *Do you have a high school diploma or equivalent? What university or college degrees do you have? Remember, some jobs will require certain degrees and it's ok to ask that on the application.*

What you may not ask: What year did you graduate high school?

6. Family Status
What you can ask: *Do you have any Commitments that might prevent you from working the assigned shifts?*

What you may not ask: Are you married? Are you single? Do you have any children?

7. Disabilities
What you can ask: *Are you able to perform all the job functions as listed in the job description?*

What you may not ask: Do you have any disabilities? Have you ever filed a worker's compensation claim? Have you ever been injured at work?

8. Convictions
It is best NOT to ask this question and not to have it on the application unless it is directly related to the position, such as a financial analyst or someone who will have a special duty, such as an attorney or an accountant. For example,

if the job requires the employee to handle money and finance, (cashier, treasurer, money transfer agent) or a job where the employee will be unsupervised and have access to all areas of the office and your customers, such as a housekeeper, custodian or property manager, as these would be considered security sensitive positions and would be permissible to ask if they have a felony conviction. You can ask any potential hire

9. Pregnancy
   Even if the pregnancy is obvious, you cannot bring it up, ever. Even if the potential hire brings it up, tread lightly and veer the interview away from the pregnancy.

   What you can ask: *How long do you plan to stay with this company? Do you have leave or vacations planned this year?*

   What you may not ask: *Are you pregnant? Are you trying to have a family? Do you plan on having children soon?*

10. Credit
    In general, do not ask questions about this unless you are sure it is permitted under the Fair Credit Reporting Act of 1970 and the Consumer Credit Reporting Reform Act of 1996. In some industries, good credit fitness is required so ask your attorney for assistance on this if you think this is a factor for you.

What you may not ask: Do you have a bank account? Do you own a home? Do you own a car? How much is your rent? Have your wages ever been garnished?

COMPLIANCE GUIDE FOR PRE-EMPLOYMENT BACKGROUND CHECKS

Background checks on employees are a good thing; you want to know who you are hiring and with whom you will share your secrets, space, and income with. However, you need to know that you cannot use the background check in such a way that would be discriminatory to your potential hire.

Certain industries will expect background checks, particularly if you're working with financial institutions. You will not be able to hire anyone who has a history of check fraud or financial crimes.

I am a firm believer in second chances and rehabilitating people who may have a criminal past and are looking to better their lives. If you have a chance to hire someone and give them a second chance without risk to your company, you should do it. Knowledge is everything; you do need to know what you are getting yourself into and make informed decisions predicated upon what is best for you and your company.

Background checks must be used in a very narrow and controlled manner, or you can get into legal trouble because there are federal laws that explicitly or implicitly apply to the practice of background investigations.

Fair Credit Reporting Act (FCRA). The federal Fair Credit Reporting Act (FCRA) regulates the use of consumer credit reports and investigative consumer reports and applies when a third-party conducts background checks on behalf of an employer. Proper written disclosure and candidate notification for this type of inquiry, required under the FCRA, should be given to the potential candidate before requesting a credit report.

First, you must give the applicant a disclosure form that informs him that you will obtain a consumer report for employment purposes. This disclosure must be a separate and standalone document that the applicant can review and execute. It may not be combined with any other document, especially and including the applicant's signed the release of liability.

Second, the applicant must sign an authorization that permits you to obtain a consumer report for employment purposes. The disclosure can only either be on a standalone form or combined with the authorization form. But if you combine them, then the combined form must not contain anything other than disclosure and authorization.

COMPLIANCE SNAPSHOT

There is no federal law that prohibits discrimination based on a criminal record.

Check your state law and verify if it does or does not prohibit discrimination based on a criminal record. If a conviction causes a disparate impact, you could be held liable for discrimination.

When terminated applicants or employees sue on these issues, they sue predicated upon discrimination for their protected class.

Documentation and a set process will stave off these potential lawsuits.

In most states, employment is "at will." This means that the employer is empowered to terminate an employee at any time for any reason so long as it is not illegal. You can use the data you receive but how you communicate the reasons for withdrawal of an offer of employment or a termination of employment should be carefully constructed to be done in a legal manner.

Anytime you are going to terminate based on the background report, you must first give a copy to the applicant/employee and allow them an opportunity to explain. This needs to be baked into the process. An applicant cannot be denied employment, and an employee cannot be terminated based on a conviction without being given a copy of the background report to review and the opportunity to explain.

If the crime relates to the applicant/employee's position directly, then after hearing the explanation you may terminate. For example, anyone with a conviction of check fraud can be denied employee or terminated from employment in any job that gives access to financial information or manages any type of account.

Arrest records may NOT be used to terminate or withdraw an offer.

Failing to disclose or putting false information on a job application also gives the tight to withdraw an offer or terminate, so ensure that you make everyone fill out an application at any level.

The purpose of the FCRA is to set national standards for screening employees; but this law only applies to background checks performed by an **outside** company, called a "consumer reporting agency" under the FCRA. The law does *not* apply in situations where the employer conducts background checks in house. The FCRA says the following *cannot* be reported:

- Bankruptcies after 10 years.
- Civil suits, civil judgments, and records of arrest, from date of entry, after seven years.
- Paid tax liens after seven years.
- Accounts placed for collection after seven years.
- Any other negative information (except criminal convictions) after seven years.

Even if you are doing your background checks in how, it really is most prudent to follow the strict guidelines set out under the FCRA to stave off frivolous lawsuits and protect yourself from inadvertently breaking a law.

Terminations need to be done is a certain way to avoid any misunderstandings regarding why an employee is being released from the company. If you can, always have a witness with you and absolutely have documentation regarding what you are terminating the employee for. If you are in a right to work state, then you can terminate for any reason but one: The WRONG reason. What that means is you need to make sure that your termination is not discriminatory or for an illegal purpose. The table below shows you the list of right to work states[6].

---

[6] https://www.ncsl.org/research/labor-and-employment/right-to-work-laws-and-bills.aspx

Currently, 27 states and Guam have given workers a choice when it comes to union membership. Labor unions still operate in those states, but workers cannot be compelled to become members as a requirement of their job. Kentucky became the 27th right-to-work state when it enacted HB 1 on Jan. 9, 2017. [7]

Before you terminate your employee, make sure you are creating documentation for the reasons you have made this decision. Your policies and procedures should include a termination and disciplinary policy. A basic sample is below.

TERMINATION AND DISCIPLINARY POLICY:

Employment with the company is at-will, which means the employment relationship may be terminated with or without cause and with or without notice at any time by you or the company. No representative of the company has the authority to enter into any agreement to the contrary. Nothing in this handbook creates an express or implied contract of employment.

The employee may be subject to disciplinary action, up to and including termination for any violations of any of the policies set forth in this employee handbook.

Employees may be terminated according to the following progressive discipline process:

First incident: Verbal Warning.

Second incident: Written Warning.

---

[7] https://www.ncsl.org/research/labor-and-employment/right-to-work-laws-and-bills.aspx

Third incident: Performance Improvement Plan with established deadlines for improvement.

Fourth incident: Termination.

However, Employer reserves the right to skip all these steps depending on the circumstances. Immediate termination will result if any of the following occur:

1. Theft.
2. Misrepresenting your time; and
3. Any harassment or breach of company policy

HR FUNCTION: MAINTAINING EMPLOYER-EMPLOYEE RELATIONS

Your human resources person, which may likely be you for the first few years of your new business, is the liaison between the employee and the employer, so wearing these two hats simultaneously can be tricky. Having an established set of rules in your employee handbook makes it easier to play these two roles. Remember, these two roles are naturally in conflict, and you must practice impartiality and patience to survive playing these parts.

Even if you are only hiring one employee, have an employee handbook ready before beginning to hire. Employees need clear direction and established rules, so they know what to do and how to behave; and employers need the structure so when an unruly or underperforming employee needs to be terminated, you have the handbook to refer to in order to show what rule or policy they violated. This protects you as the employer from any wrongful termination lawsuits.

When you hire employees, have them read and sign a document stating they have read and understand the employee handbook. Go over the basics with them so that they are aware of what is expected of them.

If you have an underperforming employee, write them up and give them a training and performance plan; try to help them get on track and give a deadline (as in a week or so) to improve on their performance. You may also terminate them but ensure you do it correctly.

If you have an employee blatantly breaking a rule, you may also terminate them immediately. Be sure you have terminated employees sign off on the termination documents you will keep in their file. If they refuse to sign, write on that document that you presented the documents and the terminated employee refused to sign. Document everything as this helps if the employee attempts to file a lawsuit. Always print out their emails and any information you have, such as social media posts, as this will help if they decide to file a lawsuit.

The very moment you decide to terminate an employee, first go and capture their social media posts and pages. After you terminate, check them again daily for a week or so to capture any posts about your company or yourself, or other employees. This is also important to have in the event they decide to sue.

HR FUNCTION: COMPENSATION AND BENEFITS

You may or may not over benefits or compensation packages depending on how large your company is, or you may only be hiring part time workers as you are still not ready for a full-time employee. Not all employers offer health insurance, 401K, or benefit packages. Some companies may offer a stipend in place of insurance or maybe not offer anything at all. If you decide to offer any type of benefits to your employees, you will likely go through a broker who will help you decide what best suits your company with respect to the number of employees you have.

As far as payroll, you will have to decide if you are going to use a professional employer organization (PEO) such as Paycom or Paychex, or if you are going to have your accounting department cut checks the old fashioned way. These are decisions that will be based on the size of your company and the number of employees that you have.

HR FUNCTION: LABOR LAW AND CONSTITUTIONAL LAW COMPLIANCE

Another function of human resource management is making sure that the company is following state and federal labor laws. They are so many aspects of the law that come into play when you begin hiring and have people working for you, so you must be aware of federal and state employment laws such as Title VII of the Civil Rights Act, the Fair Labor Standards Act, the National Labor Relations Act and many other rules and regulations. Here is a very brief overview of each law.

- **Title VII of the Civil Rights Act** protects employees and job applicants from employment discrimination based on race, color, religion, sex, and national origin.

- **The Fair Labor Standards Act (FLSA)** establishes minimum wage, overtime pay, recordkeeping, and youth employment standards affecting employees in the private sector and in federal, state, and local governments. There is no limit on the number of hours employees 16 years or older may work in any workweek.

- **The National Labor Relations Act** («**NLRA**") in was enacted by Congress in 1935 to protect the rights of employees and employers, to encourage collective bargaining, and to curtail certain private sector labor and management practices, which can harm the general welfare of workers, businesses, and the U.S. economy.

HR FUNCTION: EMPLOYEE TRAINING AND DEVELOPMENT

Training and development are two very distinct actions despite the fact the fact that they get lumped in together as one term. To clarify, employee *training* teaches your employee how to do their job according to your specifications. It may also serve to develop and improve their already existing technical skills and knowledge to do a specific job in a very specific way.

Employee development differs because it is an added value to your employee because it teaches them new skills or develops and fine tunes the ones they already have in essence, it may help them progress in their field and helps them demand more compensation in the marketplace.

Training your employees is imperative; you must at a minimum train them in how to do their job according to your rules so that they have clear expectations of what is expected of them.

Employees who also receive development opportunities are likely to be happy at work and will provide some added benefits to your workplace. Depending on how your organization is set up you may decide that development would be too costly for your company. And, if you are using a PEO, some PEO companies have free training and development for employees that may be able to be completed online during the employee's workday.

Training helps your employee provide the best service to your company and overall that saves the company a lot of money. Training also provides you, the employer, with consistent high-quality work which in turn makes the employee feel valued. Valued employees stay and then you will not continuously need to train and hire new employees for the same position. Have your employee cross train with every department in your organization to provide future opportunities and wide view of the company's objectives.

EMPLOYEE DOCUMENTS

Paperwork! Ugh. But, when you hire employees, there will be required documents that your employees must complete. There will also be documents that you should have your employees complete. Lastly, there will be documents you want your employees to complete. For example, you are required to have your employees complete Form I-9: *Employment Eligibility Verification Form*, issued by the United States Citizenship and Immigration Services (USCIS). This is required by the federal government to make sure that your employees are legally authorized to work in the United States.

You will also be responsible for withholding income taxes from your employees' paychecks, so you will need to have your employees complete IRS Form W-4, *Employee's Withholding Allowance Certificate*. You may have to have your employee complete a similar form for state income tax purposes. Then, there will be other documents that will help your employees become acclimated to your company and understand what is expected of them.

REQUIRED: EMPLOYMENT ELIGIBILITY

Form I-9

The Form I-9, Employment Eligibility Verification, is used to verify that your employees are legally allowed to work in the United States. Make sure you are using the most updated version of Form I-9 to stay compliant.

This form is divided into three sections. Your employee is responsible for filling out the first section, and you fill out the second section as the employer. There is a third section, but it is meant only for reverification of employment eligibility such as for rehires.

The form requires the employee's legal name, current address, Social Security number, and citizenship status.

The employee must bring in original documents to prove their identity and establish their employment eligibility. These are the documents you need to review and take a phot copy of so you can complete the employer section of Form I-9.

Required: New Hire Tax Forms

In order to add an employee to your payroll, you need to determine how much money to withhold from their wages for federal and, if applicable, state income taxes.

To do this, have your employee fill out two new hire tax forms: federal and your state W-4 form, if required.

Form W-4, Employee's Withholding Certificate, is required by the IRS.

Employees can add information to Form W-4 to increase or decrease their federal income tax withholding.

The W-4 asks for the employee's information, such as their Social Security number, address, marital status, and tax withholding adjustments. Employees are permitted to change their information on Form W-4 at any time throughout the year.

After you receive Form W-4 from your employee, use the tax tables in IRS Publication 15 to determine the amount of taxes to withhold from their paycheck.

State W-4

Not all states have state income tax. Alaska, Florida, Nevada, New Hampshire, South Dakota, Tennessee, Texas, Washington, and Wyoming do not have state income tax. Unless your business is in one of these states, your employee must fill out a state tax withholding form.

Like the federal W-4 form, state tax withholding forms ask employees for the same personal information. Some states use withholding allowances to determine state income tax withholding.

OPTIONAL: YOUR OWN EMPLOYMENT DOCUMENTS

In addition to employment eligibility and tax forms, you may require all new hires to fill out additional forms for your business. There are many that I think are important. Again, the more you have in writing about the policies and procedures of your company and the job description, the clearer your expectations become for your employees.

When your employee knows what is expected of them, the less issues you will experience. If you want to be able to focus on being an entrepreneur all of these documents will help you not feel like you're running a prison camp!

Offer letter: Your offer letter should be in writing. It should contain the employee's salary, whether the job is salary exempt form overtime, salary non-exempt from overtime, or hourly.

It should include the job description, the amount of vacation pay and the start date. You should also include the company's hours of operation.

Employee Agreement: This should include confidentiality clause, general statement of eligibility for benefits plan, non-compete clause, rate of pay, severability clause, specified probationary period, starting date, statement of at-will nature of employment, title of position being offered, any other state, industry-specific, or company required information, work schedule and vacation and paid time off policy. You should also include a statement indicating that there are no agreements between the parties other than those explicitly stated within the agreement.

DOCUMENTS THAT I LIKE:

- Employee Code of Conduct (if your company has a certain atmosphere of culture, this is an effective way to show them what is expected of them in the workplace, such as cleaning up after themselves in the kitchen, maintaining other common areas, social media expectations, expected atmosphere).
- Emergency Contact Form.
- Employee Handbook Acknowledgment Form.
- Benefit forms if you are going to offer life and health insurance or retirement plans.

I feel that new employees should fill out all forms at your business location on their first day. Asking them to do so prior to starting is almost like having them work before they start their employment and having you there helps them get oriented faster. But make sure they know to bring their necessary identification so you can complete their I-9 form and verify that they are allowed to work in the United States.

OTHER FORMS

You will need disciplinary forms such as write up forms, performance review forms and employee incident forms. Whenever an employee breaks a rule or violates a policy, you need to keep track of each one for termination purposes. Establishing a clear reason why an employee was terminated helps stave off sham lawsuits. You will also need termination forms, such as separation agreements, return of company property and exit interview forms.

Scan everything and keep it in a cloud file and avoid paper files if you can. Now, you have just built out your human resource department! Next, you need an employee handbook and corporate policy and procedure manual.

The Employee Handbook

Even if you are one person or only hire one person, you need a set of rules in place for employees (you are an employee too). You need an employee handbook that governs the employees as well as policies and procedures that govern the company and how the company handles issues with employees.

To develop a solid employee handbook, you need to understand the laws that govern your state, your company, and your employees. Start an outline and frame out what is important in your industry. For example, do you have special safety concerns that need to be addressed? Do you have intellectual property that needs a confidentiality clause in the handbook? Use the below as a guide but remember that employment laws can be tricky and you ALWAYS have your handbook reviewed by an employment attorney, corporate attorney or by a professional human resource management consultant.

Different state laws govern what you need to inform your employees about so make sure you consult your state laws or hire a professional to help you if you are lost in a sea of information. For example, California has a law that employers must have a written policy on anti-harassment and an internal reporting procedure).

A typical handbook would include the following information:

1. Welcome statement, mission statement, introduction
2. Equal employment opportunity statement

3. Antiharassment and antiretaliation
4. At-will nature of employment
5. Code of conduct
6. General employment information
7. Safety and security
8. Benefits (Sick leave policy, Paid vacation policy)
9. The Family and Medical Leave Act— if a business has fifty or more employees, it needs to have an FMLA policy).
10. Disclaimers—the employee manual contains policies and guidelines but is not a guarantee or contract of continuous employment. Also mention that the policies in the employee handbook can change at the employer's discretion.
11. Employee acknowledgement that they have read and will abide by the rules as stated in the handbook.

Welcome Statement, Mission Statement, and Introduction

The opening paragraph should be welcoming to the employees and let them know the items that are important to the company culture. If you have a mission statement, put it here so they can understand what the flow and personality of your company is.

For example, *"Welcome to the Entrepreneur's Law Group. We consider our employees to be our biggest asset. To help you acclimate to the company and achieve professional and personal growth, we have designed this handbook to provide the structure, rules and policies that govern the company and helped us get where we are today.*

The Entrepreneur's Law Group was founded in 2014 as a place for entrepreneurs to find the match to light the fire needed to launch into success. We are happy to have you onboard, and please know that you were chosen for the unique talents and skill set that you possess. We are honored to have you as part of this Team."

1. The Equal Employment Opportunity Statement

The purpose of equal employment opportunity (EEO) is to state frankly to your candidates and employees that your company will ensure fairness in hiring, promoting and general treatment of your employees. There are a lot of federal laws and regulations that govern companies and how they treat their employees, so be sure to discuss this with an attorney or human resource management professional. Because there are so many different forms of on-the-job discrimination, you need to keep your managers, staff members, and executives in check because ultimately the business is the one that will be sued. Training and governance are paramount. Let's start with the various laws that make up the EEO.

Title VII of the Civil Rights Act of 1964 (Title VII) makes it illegal to discriminate against a person on the basis of race, color, religion, sex, or national origin. The law also serves to protect an employee from retaliation if they complain about discrimination or participate in an EEOC proceeding, such as a discrimination investigation or lawsuit.

- **The Pregnancy Discrimination Act** amended Title VII to make it illegal to discriminate against a woman because of pregnancy, childbirth, or a medical condition related to pregnancy or childbirth.

- **The Equal Pay Act of 1963** makes it illegal to pay men and women different wages if they perform equal work in the same workplace. The law also serves to protect an employee from retaliation if they complain about discrimination or participate in an EEOC proceeding, such as a discrimination investigation or lawsuit.

- **Title I of the Americans with Disabilities Act of 1990 (ADA)** makes it illegal to discriminate against a person with a disability in private companies and state and local governments. The law also serves to protect an employee from retaliation if they complain about discrimination or participate in an EEOC proceeding, such as a discrimination investigation or lawsuit.

- **Sections 501 and 505 of the Rehabilitation Act of 1973** makes it illegal to discriminate against a person with a disability in the federal government. The law also serves to protect an employee from retaliation if they complain about discrimination or participate in an EEOC proceeding, such as a discrimination investigation or lawsuit.

- **The Age Discrimination in Employment Act of 1967 (ADEA)** protects people who are age forty or older from discrimination because of their age. The law also serves to protect an employee from retaliation if they complain about discrimination or participate in an EEOC proceeding, such as a discrimination investigation or lawsuit.

- **Title II of The Genetic Information Nondiscrimination Act of 2008 (GINA)** makes it illegal to discriminate against employees or applicants because of genetic information. Genetic information includes information about an individual's genetic tests and the genetic tests of an individual's family members, as well as information about any disease, disorder, or condition of an individual's family members (i.e., an individual's family medical history). The law also serves to protect an employee from retaliation if they complain about discrimination or participate in an EEOC proceeding, such as a discrimination investigation or lawsuit.

HERE IS A SAMPLE EEOC STATEMENT:

The Entrepreneur's Law Group is an equal opportunity employer. All aspects of employment including the decision to hire, promote, discipline, or discharge, will be based on merit, competence, performance, and business needs. We do not discriminate on the basis of race, color, religion, marital status, age, national origin, ancestry, physical or mental disability, medical condition, pregnancy, genetic information, gender, sexual orientation, gender identity or expression, veteran status, or any other status protected under federal, state, or local law.

Antiharassment and Retaliation

Your handbook will have a statement regarding the company's intolerance of harassment. The samples below are very boiler plate and should be elaborated on with respect to your state laws and your industry. A solid definition of what constitutes the different types of harassment should be included as well. Here is a very simple policy to give you an idea of what basics you should have.

Prohibited Conduct under This Policy

The Entrepreneur's Law Group, in compliance with all applicable federal, state, and local anti-discrimination and harassment laws and regulations, enforces the following anti-discrimination, anti-harassment and anti-retaliation policy in accordance with the following definitions and guidelines:

Discrimination: *The Entrepreneur's Law Group is an "equal opportunity employer." The employer will not discriminate and will take "affirmative action" measures to ensure against discrimination in employment, recruitment, advertisements for employment, compensation, termination, upgrading, promotions, and other conditions of employment against any employee or job applicant on the bases of race, creed, color, national origin, or sex.*

Sexual Harassment: Sexual harassment is a form of unlawful employment discrimination under Title VII of the Civil Rights Act of 1964 and is prohibited under The Entrepreneur's Law Group's anti-harassment policy. According to the Equal Employment Opportunity Commission (EEOC), sexual harassment is defined as "unwelcome sexual advances, requests for sexual favors, and other verbal or physical conduct of a sexual nature ... when ... submission to or rejection of such conduct is used as the basis for employment decisions ... or such conduct has the purpose or effect of ... creating an intimidating, hostile or offensive working environment."

Harassment: A sample anti-harassment policy may contain language which states:

The Entrepreneur's Law Group is committed to providing a work environment that is free from harassment. No person will be adversely affected in employment with the employer as a result of bringing complaints of unlawful harassment.

Retaliation: You need to let your employees know that they are free to bring complaints without the worry of retaliation. Sample: *We pledge that the any employee stepping forward with a complaint shall not suffer any hardship or loss for filing or responding to a bona fide complaint of discrimination or harassment, appearing as a witness during the pending investigation of a complaint, or for having served as an investigator of a complaint.*

If an employee files a bona fide complaint, it will in no way be used against the employee or have any adverse impact on the individual's status as an employee. But, please be advised that filing an unmeritorious or malicious complaint will be deemed as an abuse of this policy and will be treated as a violation. As such, an employee violating this policy will be subject to discipline, including termination.

Confidentiality: Another aspect of the complaint process that employees need to understand is that their complaint will be treated with the utmost confidentiality. A sample statement could be: *All complaints and investigations are given the highest degree of confidentiality to the extent possible, and any information that may be disclosed is done so only on a need-to-know basis. While the identity of the person making the complaint may need to be revealed to the parties involved during the investigation, we promise that the human resources manager will protect the complainant from retaliation during and after the investigation.*

You should always include a provision reading how your company will handle any complaints of harassment.

If an employee feels that he or she has been harassed on the basis of his or her sex, race, national origin, ethnic background, or any other legally protected characteristic, they should immediately report the matter to his or her supervisor. If that person is not available, or if the employee feels it would be unproductive to inform that person, the employee should immediately contact that supervisor's superior or human resources. Once the matter has been reported, it will be promptly investigated, and any necessary corrective action will be taken where appropriate. All complaints of unlawful harassment will be handled in as discreet and confidential a manner as is possible under the circumstances.

Any employee engaging in improper harassing behavior will be subject to disciplinary action, including the possible termination of employment.

AT-WILL EMPLOYMENT

Next, if your company is in an at-will employment state, you will need to include a statement regarding that as well.

The Entrepreneur's Law Group is hiring you on an "at-will" employment basis. This means that you may self-terminate your employment with us at any time with or without notice or cause. It also means that the company can terminate your employment at any time, with or without notice or cause.

Please note that as an at-will employee, you are not guaranteed that your employment shall last for any set period of time. Absent a written, valid employment agreement, no one in the company may make any representation or promise that employment is anything but "at will." Any employee, manager, or supervisor who makes such a representation or promise to you is not authorized to do so.

Code of Conduct

The code of conduct will be how you expect your employees to behave while in the office and online as well. This is a good place to incorporate your social media policy and dress code policy too and it will not only serve as a general outline of how you want your employees should behave, but also as a specific guide for handling issues in certain situations such as safety and conflicts of interest.

General Employment Information

In this section, you will discuss the "housekeeping rules" regarding use of the telephone; use of the company computer and equipment; employee-to-employee inter office relationships; drug testing; the dress code (if not already in another section); gift policy; work hours; keys; pay structure; personnel records; probation period; smoking policy; lunch policy; paid time off policy; visitors and children; timekeeping; jury duty; overtime eligibility, meal and rest periods, and exempt and nonexempt status.

Safety and Security

This section describes workplace policies that apply to everyone, such as your employees and anyone invited for business purposes on to your premises such as contractors and vendors. It will cover the policies and procedures for handling emergencies arising from fire, weather, medical issues, and workplace violence. Each employee should also sign a separate safety statement during onboarding as this can help later if there is a lawsuit.

Benefits

This section has a wide range of especially important information. It describes what your company offers to its employees as far as compensation, time off, insurance, remote work options, employee expenses, company-issued equipment, stipends for travel or cellular phone use, company car, health programs and worker's compensation information.

Most importantly, if you have more than twenty employees you need to include what is called COBRA information. COBRA stands for Consolidated Omnibus Budget Reconciliation Act, which ensures that terminated employees are eligible to receive a continuation of their group health benefits for a limited period of time after leaving your company. You only need to offer this for what is called a "qualifying event," such as termination for reasons other than gross misconduct or if you simply reduced your employee's hours to part time.

Family and Medical Leave Act (FMLA)

If you have more than fifty employees, you need to provide Family and Medical Leave Act (FMLA) leave information for your eligible employees. In addition, you should post the mandatory FMLA Notice, and all other notices required by the U.S. Department of Labor (DOL) on employee rights and responsibilities under the Family and Medical Leave Act in an area where the employees gather such as the break room, kitchen, or lounge.

In this section you will explain eligibility, the type of leave that is covered, the amount of leave the employee is entitled to, employee status and benefits while they are on leave, the employee status after leave, the use of paid and unpaid leave, and the steps they need to take to qualify and effectuate their leave. This section will also contain a statement regarding the general provisions of the Act. Again, do not try to do this on your own; at a minimum have it reviewed by an employment attorney, corporate attorney, or a professional human resource management consultant.

Disclaimers

Disclaimers are important. You have just told your employ everything that they can do; now you are telling them how they cannot use that against you later. Also, it is of most importance that you let the employee know that the handbook is NOT an employment contract. I always say that every disclaimer represents a prior lawsuit somewhere else. Here is a sample:

I understand that I am responsible for reading the handbook and adhering to all the policies and procedures of The Entrepreneur's Law Group, whether set forth in this handbook or elsewhere. I also understand that if I choose not to read this handbook, I will still be held to the policies and procedures therein and I cannot claim that I did not read the handbook as a defense of violating the company's policies and procedures.

It has been explained to me, and I fully understand, that the policies, procedures, and standard practices described in this manual are not to be considered conditions of employment. This manual does not create an express or implied contract between The Entrepreneur's Law Group and any of its employees. The Entrepreneur's Law Group reserves the right to terminate any employee, at any time, with or without notice or procedure, for any reason deemed by the company to be in the best interests of the company.

I understand that the information in this handbook is meant only as a guideline and that The Entrepreneur's Law Group may modify this handbook and any of the policies, procedures, or employee benefit programs whether described in this handbook at any time.

I understand that no manager or representative of The Entrepreneur's Law Group, other than the chief executive officer (CEO), is authorized to enter into any employment agreement on behalf of The Entrepreneur's Law Group. I also understand that any such agreement, if made, shall not be enforceable unless it is a formal written agreement signed by both me and the CEO.

I also understand that this manual is the property of The Entrepreneur's Law Group and is to be returned to the human resources department should my employment be terminated.

The Employee Acknowledgement

Now, you make the employees sign that they understand the policies and procedures. This precludes them using "I didn't know" as a defense. The acknowledgment should be saved in an employee's personnel file as this is your evidence that the employee was made aware of the policies. Again, it is imperative to have the handbook reviewed by an employment attorney, corporate attorney, or a professional human resource management consultant.

CHAPTER 14:

YOUR COMPANY'S POLICIES AND PROCEDURES MANUAL

Entrepreneurs like to be free and not bogged down by office work. If you can compile a good policy and procedure manual, then your employees will know what to do when you are out of the office. Running the business is a uniform and organized manner provides freedom so you can continue to grow, launch, and ignite new business and ideas. Once you have it done, you can use it as a template for your other businesses and just update it as needed.

A policy and procedure manual is not an employee handbook; rather it is written for the managers and supervisors as a refence tool to guide them in governing the employer-employee relationship. The employee handbook is written directly to the employees, so they know how to conduct themselves; and when they don't, the supervisor uses the policy and procedure manual to sort out the issues and make decisions that best suit the company.

First let's talk about the difference between a policy and procedure because it is quite easy to lump them together and confuse them. Simply put, a policy is a predetermined course of action to help guide managers when they are faced with a situation. The procedure is the method by which the policy is carried out. Procedures are methods—they are the way of carrying out the policy.

To illustrate, let's say have a policy that anyone who leaves the kitchen sink a mess in the shared kitchen is not allowed to use the kitchen for a week and will be written up for insubordination.

The procedure would be bringing the employee into human resources, discussing the insubordination, writing them up and then monitoring their ban from the kitchen for a week.

Your manual should be developed in keeping with your company "personality" and company "culture." You want to document the things that are the most important to the reputation of the company as well. It will be the framework of your company's management plans, company intent, business processes, emergency processes, company rules and regulations.

Also, there exists a particularly important legal aspect to a policy and procedure manual because these rules are designed to protect the legal interests of a company. The company's policies and procedures will expressly state the rights and obligations of the employees as well as the company. As such, your policy and procedure manual become the governing rules and embodiment of the employer to employee relationship.

SAMPLE POLICIES AND PROCEDURES MANUAL

Section 1. Organizational Structure and Hierarchy
This section will clearly define the executive committee, the decision makers and have the contact information for corporate headquarters and any other satellite buildings. It will break down the organization into departments and establish the leader in each department.

Section 2: Administrative Procedures
This section serves to establish policies on receipt of mail and packages as well as sending mail and packages; policies regarding equipment and the intended use of all copiers, printers, telephones and computer terminals; policies on email and internet use; accounts receivable, handling cash, use of credit cards by employees, and check requests; purchasing supplies; employee requests for accommodations and other administrative tasks as they arise.

Section 3: Facilities Management
Larger companies typically have a facilities manager that oversees the building, maintenance, the parking lot, utilities, contractions, repairs, light bulbs, janitorial and moving employees. If you are a small company, you may be leasing a space that comes with a management company and you need not worry about this section at all.

Section 4: Office Policies on Customers, Clients, Products and Services
A lot of this information will also be included in your terms of service on your webpage but having it as a separate policy is also wise. Where you will memorialize your office hours; the purchase

and refund policy; the company's privacy and confidentiality policy and how you protect customer's personal information; records retention; visitor policies and the scheduling of visitors and appointments.

Section 5: Employment and Human Resource Policies

In this section, the company's policies and procedures on human resource management will be detailed. It will include the procedures for the entire hiring process, including the initial application, background checks, interviewing process and onboarding; the creation and maintenance of personnel files and employee records; the company's Harassment policy; job descriptions; wage and salary information; pay periods and payroll procedure; performance evaluations procedure; employee attendance policy, paid-time-off policy as well as vacation, holiday and sick time policies; overtime policy, available benefits and application procedure; benefits and eligibility requirements policy; insurance procedure; office conduct policies on relationships with clients, relationships with co-workers, confidentiality and dress code; and then of course policies and procedures on disciplinary actions such as write ups and progress plans; and lastly the procedure on how to terminate an employee, the procedure for a self-terminating employee, the procedure for the employee to sign the termination documents and lastly the exit interview.

Section 6: Workplace Health and Safety

This section will clearly outline the necessary policies and procedures to keep the company, its employees, and the building safe and in good health. It will establish the emergency procedures for weather, fire, pandemics and other emergency shut downs; the policies and procedures for emergency and disaster contingency plans such as the company's server and working remotely in the event of loss of power or fire; the procedure by which accidents are reported and recorded; the policy on Workers Compensation and the procedure by which the employee engages in the process; the company's stance on smoking, drugs, alcohol and drug testing; the procedure for handling customer and client emergencies; and the policy and procedure if there is an onsite or offsite emergency after-hours.

Again, legal issues can arise very quickly, and your company's specific needs may not be mentioned in this sample list. Please make sure you consult an attorney or human resource management professional if you decide to draft your own policies and procedures.

CHAPTER 15:

WHY YOU NEED A CRM

In this digital age with everyone on the go or working remotely, any company engaging in marketing or selling needs to utilize at least one solid and multi-functional Customer Relationship Management Platform (CRM). The purpose of the CRM is to help the entire company—the sales force, client relations, managers, human resources, and marketers—communicate to each other in one place.

The is the ideal way to manage and track all external communications and relationships with each customer. The CRM will help you engage with your customers on a level unobtainable by yourself and will provide the necessary tools to build and grow your existing relationship with your customer base. Also, it helps you stay compliant because you can build in fields to indicate which customers wish to be contacted and those who have placed themselves on the do not contact list.

A good CRM needs to be multi-functional; it should store customer and prospect contact information, identify sales opportunities, record service issues, manage marketing campaigns, and track the data on every single customer interaction. If one employee leaves the company, another employee should be able to pick right up where that person left off seamlessly.

It should make all communications with that client or lead available to anyone at your company who might need it. Some features of a CRM are workflow automation, reporting customer data management, and the ability to integrate with other platforms you may be using.

A CRM also provides all the data necessary to have transparency among all departments in your company. This will only lead to increased productivity, increased conversions from lead into paying customer and help with reporting.

If everyone in your company can see how customers have been communicated with, what they've bought, when they last purchased, if they allow text messaging, you can turn a one-purchase customer into a repeat customer by cross pollinating your different departments or products to the customer.

You cannot measure what you cannot see, and you cannot grow what you are not in control of. Also, allowing a CRM to track data, messages, emails, purchases, and social media interactions builds an automatic profile of your customer base without the expense of an employee keeping manual track of orders, emails, text messages, and purchase trends.

The CRM will collect and maintain all of the data from the multiple places it usually comes from all in one place instead of allowing to float around of phones, laptops, heads, pads of paper, sticky notes and otherwise.

Some CRMs are unbelievably detailed and can be built out to your specific needs. These are going to be more costly, obviously, so start off small and increase as your needs grow. Do not go and

WHY YOU NEED A CRM

buy the most expensive one off the bat; be careful with contract commitments and be sure to think a long time about what your company needs.

Costs can range from $10.00 to $250.00 a month. There are also some free CRMs that offer extremely limited services. HubSpot, Keap, Salesforce, Zendesk and Monday.com are some of the more well-known CRMs. You get what you pay for so ensure you are choosing the right features and not overdoing it or undoing it. Data gathering is the key component to having a good CRM. When you have data on your customer's spending patterns you can create marketing strategies that speaks directly to your targeted market, but more than that, this data can also help you see where and when you are losing conversions in your sales process and sales funnels. You need to have data that shows you your exact conversion rate percentage so you can analyze and forecast future sales.

Before you choose a CRM, you need to determine what feature is most important to your sale cycle, marketing style and company communication style.

Some CRMs provide sales and marketing automation. If you are an e-commerce driven company, then you will want marketing automation tools so that you may automate aspects of your marketing. You can track your customer's progress through your sales funnels and sales process. If you don't have sales funnels, then you don't need this feature.

A CRM with analytical features will keep track of customer information and manage the processes of customer acquisition and retention. For companies they want to collect and analyze customer data for marketing other products and services, this is a great tool. The CRM should be able to track leads and convert them into customers; improve your customer's experience with the sale and follow up so you retain that customer; and manage the data of the communications between your company and the customer.

The entire purpose of the CRM is to create an easy transaction for your customers while giving you important data and analytics to acquire and retain customers, improve your sales funnels, grow, and maintain a clean text, email and telephone customer marketing list and track the progress of your sales team.

All right, so now you have the rules about marketing. You have a CRM filled or ready to be filled with your customers and leads. Let's get to digital marketing!

CHAPTER 16:

MARKETING CONCEPTS FOR ENTREPRENEURS

Marketing could truly be a book by itself so please consider looking to as many sources as you can for a full understanding of marketing and what your needs are. This chapter is only meant to show you the basic options available and to stress the importance of knowing how to communicate with your targeted customer. This is by no means an exhaustive list, rather just a primer on the types of marketing that are more commonly used.

There are a lot of theories on marketing, and you should at least be familiar with the concepts. The most basic and common theory is called the Four Pillars of Marketing, and those pillars are Product, Price, Place and Promotion.

Another common theory is called the Five Pillars of Marketing, and those pillars are Product, Price, Place, Promotion, and People.

A more comprehensive theory is the Seven Pillars of Marketing which includes Product, Price, Promotion, Place, Packaging, Positioning and People.

Let's think about why there are more factors to consider. To do that we need to travel back in time; think of your childhood whether that is in the 1940s, '50s, '60s, '70s, or '80s. Where did your parents or you buy your school clothes? Where did kids see toys that they wanted as holiday gifts? Back then the world was largely brick and mortar stores, radio commercials, television commercials and print catalogues. Business owners advertised in the newspaper, the yellow pages and on local television and radio commercials. There was also half the population of people that we have today.

The internet did more than provide a new method of communication. It homogenized us as consumers; anyone with a Wi Fi connection is a potential customer or client.

It also puts us at warp speed as we go through life cycles; we have so much information at our disposal that trends go through the entire world like wildfire. Then, it is "Next!" We are off to the next great idea.

It also created mad competition on price, service, quality, and value. People can comparison shop in seconds. You need to be on your "A" game at all times.

Because of that, the Seven Pillars of Marketing is the theory to employ to ensure that you are maximizing the information that you have so can pivot when needed.

Below is the exercise for you to complete to work through the Seven Pillars of Marketing,

Product
The product pillar is defined as the relationship between your product and the customer. The product must be something that

your customer either needs or wants. Purchases are made from a place of necessity and/or emotion.

Is your product something someone needs?

Is your product a luxury?

Is your product more likely to be purchased by the end user or as a gift?

What other products are similar to yours in the marketplace?

How is your product differentiated from comparable products?

If your product is not differentiated, how can it be? What changes can you make to make your product stand out?

Can you add a "service" feature to your tangible product, or can you add a tangible product to your service?

How does your product compare to that of the competition?

Are your products or services timely and appropriate for today's customers or have you missed a trend?"

Is there any area in your product or service where you can deliver superiority?

Pricing
Pricing involves a lot more than sticking a number on it. As we discussed in an earlier chapter, you set a price by adding all your costs together and subtracting any other sources of revenue.

That raw number is the minimum price you can charge to make a profit. Now, evaluate the demand for your product to calculate your maximum selling price. That is your price range. There are also other factors, such as cost-based pricing, demand-based pricing, competition-based pricing, psychological-based pricing, and bundled product-based pricing,

What is your price range?

What price are you charging for your product or service?

After the point of sale, is it necessary for you to provide any further service or follow-up to the customer?

Is your pricing competitive, low balled or priced as a luxury item?

Is your pricing structure appropriate for your targeted consumer?

Promotion

You should be constantly promoting and doing so from multiple channels of communication. If you are not communicating your product to the targeted consumer, how will they know you exist? They will not. Ensure that you are communicating in the right forums. If you are selling a product to senior citizens, using Snap Chat will not be beneficial. There are five basics methods of promotion, and those are Advertising, Personal selling, Sales promotion, Public relations, and Direct marketing. You should be employing all methods simultaneously.

Here are some example considerations:

Where does your targeted consumer spend the most time?

What social media platforms does your targeted consumer use?

What habits does your targeted consumer have?

Do you have an experienced social media person writing copy and posts?

What are you doing right now?

Place

You are either a brick and mortar store, e-commerce store or both. If you are a service provider, you are either home-based or based in an office.

Where you are selling depends on what you are selling. But you aren't limited to one place. If you are a brick and mortar store you should consider having an e-commerce site as well.

As an entrepreneur must make the right choice about the most beneficial places for the customer to have access to all the essential information on your product or service needed to make a buying decision.

Where are you currently selling?

Have you seen a steady increase in sales, or have they leveled off?

Where else could you sell your product or service that you currently are not doing?

Packaging

Looks matter. Not just your product, but your entire corporate image. Your posts, Your images. Your shipping materials. All your promotional materials including brochures, websites, business cards and social media accounts. The people selling your products also are part of your packaging. Their uniforms, their style, their level of neatness and good grooming. Your waiting rooms.

Basically, anything your customers see that is associated with your product or service is packaging.

You need to design the entire customer experience very carefully with that in mind, because every detail does matter, and the details can either promote your image or destroy your image.

Where are all the places where your company is visible to your customers?

Is your packaging in keeping with the image of your brand?

Did you create your packaging with your targeted consumer in mmd?

What about your packaging appeals to your targeted consumer and why?

Positioning

This is an awkward word for what it actually is. Positioning is actually how your product lives in the heart and mind of your customers. It is what they THINK and FEEL about your product. How do people think and talk about your company? What positioning do you have in your market, in terms of the specific words people use when they describe you and your offerings to others?

If you were a fly on the wall, what were customers or clients say about you?

What do think needs to be improved in your positioning?

On a scale of 1 to 10, 10 being the best, how would you rate your attention to customer needs?

How do you want your customers or clients to think about you?

What is your ideal image?

What would you consider your strongest attribute?

What is your weakest attribute?

What are three small changes that you can make today to improve how your customers feel about your company?

Do you think that your company is appealing to all its customers or clients, or just a portion of them?

<u>People</u>

Your employees, your executives, your brand ambassadors are the face of your company. They are also the ones giving out customer service, answering questions and working the hours to make sure your company is successful.

You are only as good as your worst employee.

How many employees do you have? Is that enough?

Do your employees have the right skill set?

Did your employees get the right training?

Do you have people dedicated just to customer service issues?

Do you currently have employees that you dislike?

Who is responsible for every element of your sales and marketing strategy and activities?

You need to ensure that are recruiting the right people. And, when get the right people, you need to keep them happy and treat them well, so they perform well.

Make sure each person is handling the tasks that are at their highest and best use. You should not hire an expensive marketing person and then have them answer the phone and do data entry.

Organize your staff and ensure they are performing the tasks that match their skill set.

Take the time to set up a great recruiting strategy. Ask the right questions and spend a lot of time getting to know your potential employees before you hire them.

Tips to Recruit Great Talent:

Ask your best current employees if they know anyone right for the open position

Advertise on social media platforms and post positive employee testimonials.

Advertise in multiple areas and avoid using professional recruiting agencies as they are costly and do not always have the best pool of talent.

Set up a list of questions that answer all the important questions you want to know about your candidate (but please read the chapter on what you can and cannot ask in a job interview first!)

Think of these factors in each employee: behavior, learning style, level of education, problem solving talent, decision making style, communication style, training needed and time management ability.

With these concepts in mind, you can start to frame out your digital marketing plan.

CHAPTER 17:

DIGITAL MARKETING STRATEGIES

Digital marketing is just the act of disseminating your advertising through social media, search engines, your website, Tik Tok, YouTube videos, email campaigns, Google reviews, and even mobile applications (apps) on your phone. All these platforms are your "assets."

There is no specific way to execute digital marketing strategies as each company or person has its own personality and message. In my opinion, consistency and positive messaging are key. How and when you decide to make posts will depend on your analytics and target market. This chapter covers the terminology and various strategies so you can decide what works best for you.

DEFINITIONS:

Content Marketing: Content marketing is when you create something of educational, inspirational, or informational value, like an article, video, vlog, blog, or post with relevant content to attract a particular group or audience. Some examples are podcasts, YouTube videos, infographics, article posts and eBooks. The purpose of publishing and promoting your content is to create organic traffic to your website and get more leads for the sales team. Organic traffic is any traffic that you don't have to pay for.

Inbound Marketing: Inbound marketing is a strategy that is specifically targeted to an audience that is seeking a particular solution. You post content that draws your customers to you; you create a reason for them to opt in by posting a strong message that you have information that they need and want. This kind of marketing uses a lot of different methodologies to draw in and attract your target customer.

Landing Pages: You can send your customer to a landing page to download free articles or e-books. This is where you capture their email, phone number, name, and other details. www.theEntrepreneurslaunch.com/FREEBOOK

Forms: You can exchange free content for all their demographic information. Have the targeted customer fill out the form to receive the free content and email it to them.

Website Analytics: There are so many programs that will track and follow your customer once they have been to your website.

Call to Action: These are banners and buttons that your customer clicks after interacting with your website or reading your free content. Examples are "Learn More Now" and "Buy Now."

Outbound Marketing: Outbound marketing uses all of the traditional methodologies to get your message to a large audience that may or may not need, want, or seek out your content or services. This can be mailing catalogues, flyers, using billboards, disseminating radio and print advertisements and cold calling. Think of tossing out a wide net hoping to catch a fish without knowing if there are even any fish to catch where you cast that net. It can be expensive, unproductive, hard to track and (yes, I am going to say it) old-fashioned.

Social Media Marketing: This is exactly what it sounds like: circulating content and ads on your social media platforms. You can create content to attract people to your profile and website, or you can use paid advertising which also comes with analytics. Think of content-based videos on YouTube, infographics on Instagram, articles written for LinkedIn.

Influencer Marketing: Think of all the people you know on Instagram that have 40,000 followers or more. These people are your Influencers; they have branded themselves and they have a large following and they endorse products. They get a lot of messages to collaborate with other brands—this is influencer and/or affiliate marketing. Instead of paying for traditional advertising, you pay or collaborate with the Influencer and get them to talk about your product in a Story or a post. This marketing strategy necessarily means you will also be using social media marketing and probably some content marketing too. See the big picture now?

Geofencing: Geofencing is a location-based strategy that connects you to smartphone users in a specific geographical area, such as a store, mobile applications (apps), web pages or mobile webpages. It uses tracking technology such GPS, Wi-Fi, and Bluetooth.

Click Funnels: This is an automated digital sales process that leads your customer down the sales process. It can start with an informative email, tutorials that push the customer to your website and then suggested products are presented to the prospective customer.

Search engine optimization (SEO) Marketing: SEO increases the quality and quantity of your website traffic by increasing the visibility of your website or web page. When you have a website, it doesn't mean you will show up in other people's web searches. If you "Google" the word "apple" guess what comes up? Not the fruit! In fact, there are pages and pages of Apple-related articles, blogs, advertisements, and no mention of apple the fruit because the United States Apple Association (yes, that is a real thing) didn't stand a chance against Apple without some serious SEO marketing. If you aren't visible to the various search engines (like Google) your company will not show up in the results. To find an apple on the internet you must use the words "apple fruit." When you put your word or phrase in the search engine, it goes through three stages.

THE SEARCH ENGINE DOES THE FOLLOWING:

Crawl: It will scrub the internet looking for URLs that match your query.

Index: It stores and sorts out the results from the crawling process.

Rank: It puts the results in order of relevance, meaning the best results are at the top.

Your website must have "clear navigation" and relevant URL folder structures. You want the search engine to be able to crawl inside your website too, not just find it. Your website needs Sitemaps (that is a list of URLs on your site that crawlers use to find and index your content. SEO marketing is technical and hiring someone who specializes in this is most prudent.

Your Sales Process Will Dictate Your Marketing Strategies
Understanding the sales process is important so you know when to launch these different marketing strategies. I think the most beneficial activity you can do to grow your business is marketing. It can be very costly and the most important aspect to good and solid marketing is tracking what is working and tracking what is NOT working.

There are many great sales coaches you can follow to create your own sales process, and do not ever recommend copying someone else's methods for two reasons. 1. It could cause legal issues and 2. It is better to be different and carve out your own unique personality in the sea of sales coaches and trainers.

This information is NOT meant to teach you the skills of a great salesperson as I am certainly not qualified to teach you anything about how to sell. This is only meant to show what the stages of the sale are, so you determine when and how to market to your customer.

A typical sales process is Prospecting, Preparation, Approach, Presentation, Handling Objections, Closing, and Follow-up.

Prospecting is finding your targeted customer. You should be hard at work creating customer profiles, identifying the people you want to contact and then producing creative ways to contact them.

Preparation takes the time to evaluate your customer and figure out the best method to attract their attention. Email? Phone? Cold call? Text message?

Approach is when you attempt to make contact or make that c9ontact. Mostly likely, this is not the sale, but the warming up of the relationship.

Presentation is your chance to shine. You may only get one bite of the apple so make it spectacular.

Handling Objections is telling the customer why they should buy no matter what their objection is. You need to be prepared to come back with a reason that their objection is "overruled."

Closing is when you make the sale, and the contract is signed, and money is exchanged. This is the BEST time to make sure you leave the best impression so you can start selling them something else.

Follow up is when you call your customer to make sure they are happy with the product or service. If they are, have them right a review (digital marketing asset if it is online) and ask for referrals too.

How do you know if all this marketing is even working? Analytics. Key Performance Indicators. Having a sold digital marketer, you can trust.

A Key Performance Indicator (KPI) is a measurable value that demonstrates how effective the business's objectives are and they should be utilized at many different levels and stages in order to paint a picture of the company's success in reaching its targets.

A KPI needs to be measurable, must have a target, must have a clearly defined data source, and should be reported frequently and consistently.

This all sounds very professional and great, but what the hell does it mean?

If you are in sales, examples of KPIs are the dollar value of contracts executed; net sales, number of click conversions, number of new contracts signed per month, average time to convert a lead into a sale.

Some examples of finance KPIs are revenue growth, net profit margin, gross profit margin, cash flow, account receivables, and turnover.

Examples of marketing KPIs are monthly website traffic, e-books published, vlogs published, conversion rate on your call-to-action campaigns and number of qualified leads received.

These KPIs are all measurable and give a clear picture of the company's growth. This is the only way you will know your marketing strategies are working.

I will say it again—you cannot measure what you cannot see, and reporting is literally everything. That is where your KPIs come in.

CHAPTER 18:

KEY PERFORMANCE INDICATORS

K PIs are quantifiable measures used to evaluate the success of an organization, a team, or an individual in achieving specific objectives. They are used to monitor performance, track progress, and make informed decisions. KPIs can vary depending on the industry, organization, and goals. I know you are thinking that I just said a whole lot of nothing, but it will all make sense by the end of the chapter. Basically, it is just reporting on what works and what didn't work. Here are some common types of KPIs and how they are used:

1. Financial KPIs: These KPIs focus on financial performance, such as revenue, profit margins, return on investment (ROI), and cash flow. They help assess the financial health of a business, measure profitability, and guide financial decision-making.

2. Operational KPIs: These KPIs measure the efficiency and effectiveness of operational processes within an organization. Examples include production output, cycle time, customer complaints, and on-time delivery. They help identify bottlenecks, optimize operations, and improve overall performance.

3. Customer KPIs: These KPIs evaluate customer satisfaction, loyalty, and overall customer experience. Examples include customer retention rate, Net Promoter Score (NPS), customer complaints, and customer lifetime value. They provide insights into customer preferences, help identify areas for improvement, and gauge the success of customer-centric strategies.

4. Sales and Marketing KPIs: These KPIs track sales and marketing performance. Examples include sales revenue, conversion rate, lead generation, customer acquisition cost (CAC), and marketing return on investment (ROI). They measure the effectiveness of sales and marketing efforts, guide resource allocation, and inform strategic decisions.

5. Employee KPIs: These KPIs assess individual and team performance within an organization. Examples include employee productivity, absenteeism rate, training hours, and employee satisfaction. They help measure workforce effectiveness, identify training needs, and support performance management.

6. Quality KPIs: These KPIs measure the quality and reliability of products or services. Examples include defect rate, customer complaints related to quality, and adherence to quality standards. They assist in identifying quality issues, implementing improvement initiatives, and ensuring customer satisfaction.

7. Sustainability KPIs: These KPIs focus on environmental and social sustainability. Examples include energy

consumption, waste reduction, carbon emissions, and diversity metrics. They help organizations monitor their environmental impact, social responsibility, and progress towards sustainability goals.

It's important to note that the selection of KPIs should be aligned with the organization's goals, strategies, and industry standards. KPIs should be specific, measurable, achievable, relevant, and time-bound (SMART) to effectively track progress and drive performance improvement.

Businesses need Key Performance Indicators (KPIs) for several reasons:

1. Goal Setting: KPIs help businesses set specific, measurable goals and objectives. They provide a clear direction for the organization and help align the efforts of different teams and departments towards a common purpose.

2. Performance Measurement: KPIs provide a means to measure the performance and progress of a business against its goals. By tracking relevant metrics, businesses can assess their performance and identify areas of improvement or success.

3. Decision Making: KPIs offer valuable insights that can aid in decision-making processes. They provide data-driven information about the business's performance, allowing managers and leaders to make informed choices about resource allocation, strategy adjustments, and priority setting.

4. Accountability: KPIs establish accountability within an organization. They help define roles and responsibilities by assigning specific metrics to different individuals or teams. By monitoring KPIs, businesses can hold employees accountable for their performance and drive a culture of responsibility.

5. Continuous Improvement: KPIs play a crucial role in fostering a culture of continuous improvement. By regularly tracking performance metrics, businesses can identify inefficiencies, bottlenecks, or areas that require optimization. This enables them to make necessary adjustments, implement process enhancements, and drive ongoing improvement efforts.

6. Performance Alignment: KPIs facilitate alignment across different levels of the organization. When everyone is working towards the same set of performance indicators, it ensures that individual efforts and departmental objectives are in line with the overall strategic goals of the business.

7. Communication and Transparency: KPIs provide a common language and framework for communication. They allow businesses to communicate their performance to stakeholders, shareholders, employees, and customers in a concise and understandable manner. Transparently sharing KPIs fosters trust, facilitates collaboration, and enhances the overall effectiveness of communication within and outside the organization.

KPIs are not just essential but necessary for businesses as they provide a means to set goals, measure performance, make informed decisions, establish accountability, drive continuous improvement, align efforts, and communicate effectively. They are a vital tool for monitoring and optimizing business performance in various areas such as sales, marketing, finance, operations, and customer service. Imagine if you had a $10,000 advertising spend that resulted in zero revenue? KPIs prevent that from happening. Also, what if you started a whole new customer service approach and invested time and money into training and software and people were still having difficulty in getting a resolution. Again, KPIs can save the day.

Businesses track Key Performance Indicator (KPI) data through a combination of manual and automated processes. This will make you understand what exactly a KPI is and how to use it, so here are some common steps involved in tracking KPI data:

1. Identify and define KPIs: Determine the specific metrics that are important for measuring performance and achieving business objectives. These could include financial indicators, customer satisfaction scores, sales targets, website traffic, or employee productivity.

2. Set targets and benchmarks: Establish realistic targets or benchmarks for each KPI. These targets function as a reference point for measuring progress and performance.

3. Data collection: Gather relevant data to measure the KPIs. This can involve manual data entry, integration with existing systems (such as sales software, CRM systems, or website analytics tools), or the use of specialized tools or software designed for KPI tracking.

4. Data storage and organization: Create a structured system for storing and organizing the collected data. This can be in the form of spreadsheets, databases, or dedicated business intelligence (BI) tools.

5. Data analysis: Analyze the collected data to assess performance against the defined KPIs. This involves examining trends, patterns, and variations to identify areas of improvement or concern.

6. Reporting and visualization: Present the analyzed data in a clear and understandable format. This can be achieved through reports, dashboards, charts, or graphs, which allow stakeholders to quickly grasp the current status of the KPIs.

7. Regular monitoring and review: Continuously monitor the KPIs to track progress over time. Regularly review the data and compare it against the established targets or benchmarks. This enables businesses to identify areas that require attention and make informed decisions based on the insights gained.

8. Adjust and optimize: If the data indicates a need for improvement, take action to address any issues or inefficiencies identified. This may involve making changes to processes, strategies, or resource allocation to optimize performance and work towards achieving the desired targets.

It's worth noting that the specific methods and tools used to track KPI data can vary depending on the nature and scale of the business. Many organizations leverage specialized software solutions, such as business intelligence platforms, data analytics tools, or integrated performance management systems, to streamline and automate the KPI tracking process.

I am not going to tell you that a business can't potentially grow if they don't use KPIs, but it may be more challenging to measure and track its progress effectively. Even if they grow, what is they could have grown more? What if they just got lucky the first year? KPIs are widely used in businesses to assess performance, set goals, and make data-driven decisions. They provide a quantitative and measurable way to evaluate various aspects of a business's operations, such as sales, revenue, customer satisfaction, employee productivity, and more.

However, it's worth noting that KPIs are not the only means of managing and growing a business. Some businesses may rely on alternative methods of measurement and assessment, such as qualitative feedback, customer testimonials, market research, or industry benchmarks. These approaches can provide valuable insights and guide decision-making, even if they are not as quantifiable as traditional KPIs.

Ultimately, whether a business chooses to use KPIs or not, it is crucial to have some form of performance measurement and tracking in place to ensure continued growth and success. That's your decision, and I vote for KPIs even if they are on a small scale to start.

So, when should you start? Now! While businesses should start using KPIs as early as possible in their operations because implementing them early on establishes a solid framework for measuring and evaluating performance against set goals and objectives. There is always no time like the present. The specific timing may vary depending on the size, nature, and industry of the business, but here are a few key points to consider:

1. Early stages: Even during the early stages of a business, it is important to define clear goals and objectives. By establishing KPIs early on, businesses can track progress, identify areas for improvement, and make informed decisions. This helps create a culture of performance measurement and accountability from the start.

2. Growth phase: As a business grows, KPIs become even more crucial. They enable organizations to monitor various aspects of their performance, such as sales, revenue, customer satisfaction, operational efficiency, and employee productivity. KPIs provide valuable insights into the effectiveness of strategies and initiatives, helping businesses make data-driven decisions and course corrections as needed.

3. Strategic planning: KPIs play a vital role in strategic planning. By aligning KPIs with the overall business strategy, organizations can ensure that their efforts are focused on the most critical areas. KPIs provide benchmarks against which progress can be measured, facilitating strategic adjustments and resource allocation to achieve long-term objectives.

4. Continuous improvement: KPIs are not static; they evolve as businesses mature. By regularly reviewing and refining KPIs, organizations can adapt to changing market

conditions, industry trends, and internal dynamics. This enables continuous improvement and ensures that the KPIs remain relevant and aligned with the business's evolving priorities.

Implementing KPIs helps establish a culture of performance measurement, enables data-driven decision-making, supports strategic planning, and fosters continuous improvement throughout the business's lifecycle. This is how you scale and provide lifetime value to your products and services.

Now because you have a marketing plan, including KPIs, it is time for me to lecture you on compliance.

CHAPTER 19:

MARKETING RULES AND THE LAW

There are so many governing agencies, laws, regulations and Acts for businesses, employees, the internet, the transactions, and the communication systems, as well as strict rules for cold calling, emailing, texting and your web page terms and conditions and privacy policy. Welcome to marketing in the digital age.

The purpose of this chapter is to familiarize you with the governmental agencies that regulate marketing and advertising and to teach you the specific rules and regulations that govern marketing and advertising. Due to the heavy social media marketing that drives most companies these days, there is an emphasis on online marketing and advertising, including text message campaigns. This chapter covers the regulations for the content you will be creating for your business as well as the method by which your content will be disseminated.

Many companies sell to both businesses and consumers. The laws that protect consumers are very different and are more stringent than the laws that protect companies so selling a product to an individual is very different that selling it to a large corporation. The laws are designed to protect people, not companies, so Consumer Rights Laws are heavily regulated, and transactions are heavily policed. Whenever you are creating an advertisement always consider:

1. Who is my ultimate customer? (Individual or a company)
2. How is the marketing content being disseminated? (Web ad or direct email)
3. Is the purpose of the content to be informative or persuasive as if to sell a product or service?
4. Have all the numbers and data been verified?
5. Are there any "plays on words" or claims that require a disclaimer?

What we need to worry about most: telling a customer anything that isn't 100% true (which is considered deceptive practices) in order to get them to buy a product or service. That can either be a blatant lie or even just a small word to make it misleading.

Using clever plays on words, analogies, metaphors, or phrasing things to trick the mind or eye are all methods that could be construed as deceptive or false advertising.

So, who is watching and monitoring what we do? Well, probably no one. What happens is customers start complaining to the company first and then they make formal complaints. Once that happens, then the governmental agencies that are tasked with protecting the public from false and misleading advertising start an investigation.

There are several different agencies that govern advertising and communication methods by which we publish and disseminate the content. Then there are Acts, which are the laws enacted by Congress or the Legislature that give the federal agencies the right to prosecute offenders.

FTC–THE FEDERAL TRADE COMMISSION

The Federal Trade Commission Act allows the FTC to act in the interest of all consumers to prevent deceptive and unfair acts or practices. The Commission, which is made up of 5 people nominated by the President of the United States and confirmed by the Senate, have determined that a representation, omission, or practice is *deceptive* if it is likely to mislead consumers and affect consumers› behavior or decisions about the product or service. That is a very broad statement, and the FTC has quite a bit of power. So, when drafting and creating advertisements for your company, be very careful to not mislead with facts or mislead by leaving facts OUT. An example of this is advertising something for free when the consumer must pay shipping or pay undisclosed charges to receive the free item.

Also, any claims that you make must be **substantiated**, especially when they concern health, safety, or performance. The type of evidence may depend on the product, the claims, and what experts believe necessary. If you say your product helps people lose weight, you need to have data and case studies to back up that claim.

Here are examples of companies that were found guilty of false advertising:

- ✓ Activia yogurt–Dannon stated that its yogurt had nutritional benefits other yogurts didn't. They had to pay $45 million in a class action settlement.
- ✓ Splenda–Ads say it is made from sugar; but that is not the case.
- ✓ Eclipse Gum–Said it killed germs in your mouth.

- ✓ Red Bull: The slogan said Red Bull could "give you wings"—cost them $13 million because a consumer sued after they didn't sprout wings. No joke.
- ✓ Oil of Olay: touched up a photo of a model in an anti-aging beauty crème ad.

Companies are heavily responsible for claims they make about their products and services. Third parties—such as advertising agencies or website designers and catalog marketers—may also be liable for making or disseminating deceptive representations if they participate in the preparation or distribution of the advertising or know about the deceptive claims. So, if you hired an agency to create your content and you know it is misleading, you cannot simply pass the buck. You are still on the hook.

Just like companies, content creators and website designers are responsible for reviewing the information used to substantiate ad claims once a company hires them. The FTC will determine to what extent the agency participated and determine whether the agency knew or should have known that the ad included false or deceptive claims.

Disclaimers and disclosures must smack the customer in the face. Any demonstration must be real and show how the product will perform under normal use. Any, if you promised a refund or money back guarantee, then you are obligated to give the money back to the consumer if they ask for it.

THE FTC AND ONLINE ADVERTISING

The FTC act's prohibition on "unfair or deceptive acts or practices" widely covers advertising claims as well as marketing and promotional activities. It even covers sales practices. The act is not limited in what kind of content it covers—it covers any and all communications that advertise to consumers, such as all methods of advertising, marketing, and sales online, as well as the same activities in print, television, telephone, and radio. The commission has brought countless lawsuits to stop companies from making false claims.

CLEAR AND CONSPICUOUS DISCLOSURES IN ONLINE ADVERTISEMENTS

You cannot say something that is purposely misleading or untrue to catch attention and then have a disclaimer below; you cannot disclaim away a lie or omission. The real purpose of a disclaimer is to "qualify" or "limit" a claim to avoid a misleading impression. Just remember that a disclaimer can never ever cure a false claim. If a disclosure is required, it must be clear and conspicuous.

When it comes to online ads, the basic principles of advertising law apply:

1. Advertising must be truthful and not misleading.
2. Advertisers must have evidence to back up their claims ("substantiation").
3. Advertisements cannot be unfair.

PROXIMITY AND PLACEMENT OF YOUR DISCLOSURE

The disclosure must be near the phrase that you are disclaiming. Proximity increases the likelihood that consumers will see the disclosure and relate it to the relevant claim or product which makes the FTC very happy.

TESTIMONIALS AND ENDORSEMENTS

Testimonials and endorsements must reflect the *typical* experiences of consumers unless the ad clearly and conspicuously states otherwise. A statement that not all consumers will get the same results is not enough to qualify a claim. Testimonials and endorsements can't be used to make a claim that the advertiser itself cannot substantiate.

Connections between an endorser and the company that are unclear or unexpected to a customer also must be disclosed, whether they have to do with a financial arrangement for a favorable endorsement, a position with the company, or stock ownership. Expert endorsements must be based on appropriate tests or evaluations performed by people that have mastered the subject matter.

THE COST OF NONCOMPLIANCE

The FTC periodically joins with other law enforcement agencies to monitor the Internet for potentially false or deceptive online advertising claims.

If your advertisements don't comply with the law, you could face enforcement actions or civil lawsuits. For advertisers under the FTC's jurisdiction that means they can be given a legal order to cease and desist, with fines up to $42,530 per violation if they keep publishing the infringing advertisement. Companies can receive injunctions by federal district courts that make them close their businesses and lose everything; then they sell off the business assets to force the company to pay back anyone who bought their products under a claim of false advertising.

FCC—THE FEDERAL COMMUNICATIONS COMMISSION

CONSENT. Burn that in your brain because it is the most important word in digital marketing as far as texting and emailing. Customer consent is the key to email and text marketing laws. Text and email marketing can make a huge impact on your business when executed correctly, and that means getting proper customer consent. Not only is customer consent required by FCC regulations, but it's also a marketing best practice in a world filled with spam.

So as an entrepreneur, you want to know "when can I text my customers?" According to FCC rules, when they affirmatively opt in and check a box. When they text you to opt in. Without exception, consent for commercial text messaging must be in writing and cannot be given verbally. Just remember the number one rule in SMS marketing laws is "clear and documented customer consent."

WHO REGULATES SMS TEXT MESSAGE MARKETING?

There are three primary organizations that weigh in on text marketing rules and regulations; however, they all carry different powers and different levels of influence on what can and can't be done. Much of the confusion that companies and entrepreneurs experience about the ins and outs of text message regulations comes from not understanding the influence, powers, or relationships between these three groups. So, the power players are:

1. **CTIA** (Cellular Telecommunications Industry Association) This association is comprised of wireless carriers and other influential members that help enforce best practices. Because they are not a government agency, they cannot pass or enforce laws; however, they have the power to

shut down long code / short code messages and block text messaging services for groups they find to be non-compliant. That is serious power.

2. **FCC** (Federal Communications Commission)
The FCC is a government organization and therefore can create and enforce laws that are suitable for fines and legal action. They oversee the Telephone Consumer Protection which deals with unwanted phone calls and text messages.

3. **MMA** (Mobile Marketing Association)
The MMA is an influencer but not an enforcer. The MMA has no legal enforcement abilities like the FCC, and they do not have the CITA's control over messaging or power to block messages. They help determine what best practices are for the regulations while making sure consumers still get the information that they want from effective policies.

COMPLIANCE SNAPHOT: THE TCPA AND TEXTING

Checklist:

1. **Consent.** (1) Always get a consumer's written consent before sending any text messages for commercial or marketing purposes. You will need to show that the consumer received "clear and conspicuous disclosure" of what messages they'll be receiving; and that they clearly agreed to receive text messages by checking the box next to the opt-in language. **Tax-exempt nonprofit organizations are not required to comply with the do-not-call provisions of the TCPA.

2. **Always have an Auto Opt-Out mechanism.** Recipients must be able to opt-out of receiving text messages by replying directly to the text message.

3. **Identify the sender.** The TCPA dictates that text messages must include (1) the identity of the entity sending the text and (2) opt-out instructions. Then, CTIA further insists that messages must include opt-out instructions at least monthly!

4. **Always text during appropriate times.** Text messages for marketing purposes can only be sent between the hours of 8 am and 9 pm (local time of the receiver). Also, the TCPA disallows text messages sent to a mobile phone from an auto-dialer (including text message marketing) unless (1) the consumer previously opted in or (2) if the message is sent for emergency purposes.

CHECKLIST FOR AUTOMATIC TEXT MESSAGE CAMPAIGNS

1. **Opt-in consent required.**

2. **Opt-out mechanisms** required. A consumer must be able to opt out with any of the universal keywords; STOP, END, CANCEL, UNSUBSCRIBE, and QUIT. Recurring-messaging programs are also required to have opt-out instructions at regular intervals, at least once per month. You can send one final opt-out message to confirm that a user has opted out successfully.

3. **Customer Care**. You have to provide a "customer care clause" so recipients can find out more about what you're texting about and who you are.

4. **Opt-in Confirmation Message. You are required to send a c**onfirmation text is required after opt-in to show:
   a. The identity of the sender
   b. Customer care information (examples include reply help for help, contact us at 888-888-8888, email support at support@gmail.com, etc.)
   c. Opt-out instructions (reply STOP to unsubscribe)
   d. Messaging/product quantity or recurring-messages disclosure
   e. "Message and data rates may apply" disclosure.

5. **Privacy Policy**. You need to have a privacy policy that provides up-to-date information such as details on help keywords and opt-out keywords, and the like.

6. **Consistency.** When you receive an opt-in, it is only for that program or campaign; you can't switch to t a new one. So, keep your name consistent from the call-to-action, the privacy policy, and every single message that is sent.

7. **Requirements in the Call-to-Action.** Because the call-to-action is the place where customers sign up for messages, it is literally your front porch, and this is where you put the best stuff. You must have:
    a. Messaging frequency or recurring messages disclosure
    b. Terms and conditions or link to terms and conditions
    c. Product description
    d. Privacy policy or link to privacy policy
    e. STOP keyword (this can appear on a separate page in the terms and conditions)
    f. "Message and data rates may apply" disclosure

COMPLIANT OPT-IN STRATEGIES: HOW TO BUILD A CLEAN TEXT MARKETING LIST

Include Opt-In Language inside our Agreements
We can obtain consent by getting people to opt-in inside our Agreements. We can add the appropriate TCPA-consent language at the end to receive offers and products and updates.

Direct Signatures at Events
Paper or digital (tablet) forms for text messaging consent can be made available at events on signup sheets, refund forms, offers, order forms, anywhere we can interact directly with customers/

prospects. The form must include the appropriate wording so that customers know exactly what they are signing.

Banner Announcement on Web and Mobile

Add a call-out banner or pop-up banner that is visible on every page of our website.

Send out Text Campaigns so they Opt-in

We must have the appropriate response when the prospect/customer texts us. They need to know they opted-in and can opt-out.

Use Smart Buttons on the websites

You can connect any call-to-action button (like "Buy Now") can now be connected to an automated opt-in process. This includes your 'apply online', 'become a member', or even a 'chat with us' button.

SMS Marketing Program

Offer free digital content if someone opts-in via text message. A sample would be to advertise on social media or via email and have customers and prospects text "FREE" to 313131.

The Telemarketing Sales Rule[8]

The FTC created the Telemarketing Sales Rule (The "TSR") to protect consumers from aggressive telemarketers, scammers and to protect consumer's privacy rights. Businesses that violate the TSR are subject to fines of up to $11,000 per violation. The FTC defines telemarketing as *"any plan, program or campaign to induce the purchase of goods, services, or a charitable*

---

[8] https://www.ftc.gov/tips-advice/business-center/advertising-and-marketing/telemarketing

contribution over the telephone."[9] The TSR prohibits telemarketers from making misrepresentations and requires them to give the consumer certain disclosures.

The TSR was amended in 2003 to include the Do Not Call Registry which was contemporaneously established with the help of the FCC. The purpose of the Do Not Call list was to attempt to reduce telemarketing calls consumers receive at home. Now, if a telemarketer calls a consumer at home, they are breaking the law and can be fined a lot of money.

The TSR requires multiple disclosures that need to be given before any promotional language is initiated. If you are making outbound calls, your telemarketer needs to:

- Identify the Company/Seller.
- Identify that the purpose of the call is to sell.
- Identify the products or series they are trying to sell.
- The cost of price of the goods or services they are selling.
- The existence of any restrictions, limitations, or conditions; and
- The refund or no-refund policy.

A telemarketer cannot:

- Call again if the consumer asked to be taken off the marketing list.
- Call anyone on the Do Not Call Registry.
- Call before 8:00 AM or after 9:00 PM in the consumer's time zone.

---

[9] https://www.ftc.gov/tips-advice/business-center/advertising-and-marketing/telemarketing

- Make any misrepresentations or false statements.
- Ask for payment for any services not delivered such as credit repair, recovery room or advance fee loan or credit services.

Of course, there are exceptions to the rule, but they are narrowly construed so tread lightly.

These are the exceptions:

- Calls made by the consumer is response to your advertisement as long as it is not about investment opportunities; credit repair services; recovery services; or loans or other extensions of credit, the granting of which is represented (or misrepresented) to be guaranteed or highly likely.
- Calls made by consumers in response to direct mail advertising if the advertising discloses all the material information as specifically required by the TSR.
- Catalog sales.
- Calls made by the consumer directly to you.
- Calls involving incomplete sales.
- Calls that are Business-to-business calls (unless nondurable office or cleaning supplies are being offered).
- Calls that are made for the sale of pay-per-call services and/or the sales of franchises.

Business to Business (B2B)

If you are calling a business and the person who answers the phone declines the sale because the business has no need for the product, you cannot then attempt to sell that product to the individual—this would violate the TSR.

Also, keep in mind that B2B calls are NOT exempt from complying with the FCC's wireless dialing rules when using an automatic telephone dialing system. The TCPA rule against calling cell phone numbers with automatic telephone dialing systems applies to B2B calls.

So again, CONSENT is key. Make sure you have prior express consent before contacting any businesses using an automatic telephone dialing system. Just because a business may advertise their phone number online does not mean that they are consenting to receiving robocalls or auto dialers.

Telemarketers relying on the B2B exemption must ensure that they do not transition sales efforts to target the individual answering the call when the "business" states that it does not have a need for the product or service being sold.

When telemarketers attempt to sell to individuals any products that are suitable for either business or personal uses, they must comply with the National DNC Registry, satisfy disclosures requirements, abide by internal suppression lists, comply with calling time curfews and abandonment rates, and ensure that caller ID information is properly transmitted.

Keep in mind, this is all federal law. Guess what? Some states have even more stringent rules against telemarketing. Many other states have telemarketing rules that are significantly more stringent than federal law.

Although some B2B telemarketing calls are exempt from the national Do Not Call list law, not every state exempts B2B telemarketing calls under state law. In various jurisdictions, B2B telemarketers must also register and place a bond prior to calling to or from those states.

Interestingly, the TSR was also recently clarified in other respects:

- Any recording made to memorialize a customer's or donor's express verifiable authorization is required to "clearly and conspicuously" state an accurate description of the goods, services, or charitable contribution prior to accepting payment. The seller and/or telemarketer bear the burden of proving that exemptions apply.
- Do Not Call Registry fees cannot be shared among numerous sellers.
- The types of unlawful burdens that interfere with a consumer's right to be added to an internal DNC list were clarified.

Make sure you scrub your marketing lists frequently; "purge" before you "merge" any lists in your CRM, do checks against the Do Not Call Registry at least once a month, and take compliance very seriously.

Now, if you do have an established relationship with a business or a consumer, you can call for up to eighteen months after their last purchase, payment, or delivery—even if their number is on the National Do Not Call Registry. If a consumer or business makes an inquiry or submits an application to a company, you can call them for up to ninety days (three months) afterward.

Utilizing a multi-functional CRM that tracks opt-ins for texting and calls as well as having a compliance checkup from your attorney can stave off a lot of legal trouble and save you money.

CHAPTER 20:

THE SALES CYCLE

I am by no means a sales professional, but from a legal and business standpoint, I understand the sales cycle. Each cycle has a specific purpose, and every personality has a different approach to how they close a sale. This chapter is not about telling you how to sell because it's not my wheelhouse and there are many coaches and influencers who you can follow and learn from. The purpose of this chapter is to get you familiar with the basic sales cycle from a business perspective because I firmly believe that every profession or trade needs to know how to sell—it is obviously not all about exchanging money for a product or service. It is about an exchange of something of value to one person for something of value from the other person. Understanding the framework of a sale is important even if it is just to get someone to do something for you—like invest in your idea or agree with your perspective.

A sales cycle has seven distinct stages with a different purpose. Some of the stages will overlap, but mostly it is important to respect the cycle and purposes of the stages. There is not a lot of new material on this as it is time tested and most gurus follow the same methods. I will say it is personality and approach that make the difference, so pick the sales guru that you relate to the most for those techniques.

1. PROSPECT

Think of a gold miner standing in the mountains overwhelmed about where to start digging. Those gold miners did not just start swinging on the first rock they saw. They looked around, did a little planning to see if it was worth digging in. They panned out the dirt and moved on quicky if they did not see evidence of any gold.

That is you, sitting in front of your computer trying to figure out how to connect with your potential customers. You need to seek them out and try to communicate with them.

That is called prospecting! You're going out and finding YOUR gold which is potential buyers, customers, or clients.

You may have the greatest idea, the most elite service or most stellar product in the universe, but without buyers, customers, or clients, it does not matter. You need to connect with the people who have the problem that your product or service solves.

Write your answers to these questions to help you narrow your audience. You need to know:

1. How is your product or service differentiated from others on the market? What is the most unique feature?

2. Does your product or service clearly define the problem it solves? What problem does it solve?

3. How will your product or service improve someone's life or business?

4.   Why would someone buy your product or service over another product with the same features?

Lead generation is a lot like panning through the dirt. You need to soft through large groups of people to find your gold nuggets. Offering informational content is a great way to attract your customers directly to you. Bam. Golden nuggets in your inbox. These are the people that you would add to your CRM for marketing. Look at it this way; your content is the shimmery attention-getter that leads them to your page. You must capture them. Imbed a link in your social media posts that bring the prospects to your website. Then, you have a lot of options on how to capture their information. Some examples are below:

1.   Have them fill out a submission form so they can receive information regarding the post that brought them to your page.

2.   Have them fill out a submission form so they can receive a fee newsletter.

3.   Have them fill out a submission form so they can schedule a call.

4.   Have them text you to opt-in to text marketing by offering a discount code or free content on social media.

Now you have the leads to add to your CRM. Also, contemplate automating the next steps.

2. FIRST CONTACT

Now that you have created a marketing list for potential customers you have to carefully plan your first contact. This can be done via email, text message, phone call or targeted social media post. This will depend on what your industry is and what your product is. Keeping that in mind, this first contact is to create a "warm" relationship, it is not by any means the time to make a full-blown sales pitch.

The whole point of the first contact is to "warm" up your prospect and see if they are interested in your type of product or service. The phone is the best way to cover a lot of territory and churn through your leads quickly. You can set appointments to make your full sales pitch, invite them to an event, offer a discount for a future purchase or simply just introduce yourself and let them know that you have a product or service that will solve their problem.

Always have full data on who you are calling, the more you know the better chance you have of converting your prospect into a client.

If you obtain key information about them, you can have a high-quality call and keep their attention. It is all about keeping them engaged, and you can do that by appearing interested and knowing sone things about them to strike up a meaningful conversation.

You should always write down what you are going to say first. There are plenty of companies and software programs that generate cold calling scripts, and you can find dozens online for free.

Or you can use this format and write your own.

Introduction: Hi Byer! This is Hunter with The Law Group. Hope you are having a great day!

Connecting Statement: I saw that recently incorporated your Start Up and I wanted to say congrats.

Reason for Calling: I see that you are in the retail industry, and I wondered if you had any compliance concerns for your online sales strategies.

Qualifying Statement: Yes, that is something I hear all the time. There are lot of state and federal regulations that can be kind of confusing and there is no way to automate the compliance aspect, you must build it into your process. That can be overwhelming when you are trying to get up and running.

Your "Ask": Byer, I am so glad we got to connect today, and I think you could benefit from a compliance tune up. I don't want to take up too much of your time today so can I set up a time with you to do a demo with you on Zoom?

Always keep in mind that the goal of a cold call is not to pitch to someone on the spot. You're just trying to get them to commit to a meeting later so you can do a full sales pitch. This call should be filled with energy, be brief and leave your prospect feeling excited, not ambushed.

3. QUALIFY THE LEADS: TURN LEADS INTO CUSTOMERS

Qualifying your leads is an organic process and you will do this from your own research, the first initial cold call or contact and some all the way through the sales pitch. Unless you qualify your leads early in the process, you may end up pursuing buyers, customers or clients who will never spend money on you because they do not need or want your product. What this really means is you are panning again and sifting out the fool's gold, dirt, and sand in search of the golden nuggets. Simply put, in this process, you need to find the decision maker who needs your product and has the ability and finances to buy it. Sounds simple, but it really is not. Here are some questions you can ask your potential customer to see if they are worth continuously pursuing:

1. How could this product help you?
2. How would this product impact your daily life?
3. What problems are you experiencing right now?
4. How would this product help alleviate the problems you are experiencing right now?
5. Are you able to approve purchases like this?
6. Is this purchase within your budget?
7. Can this product reach you logistically?

The whole point of this step is to prevent you from exhausting your resources on people who cannot or will not purchase your products or services.

4. PRESENT YOUR PRODUCT

Now it is time to demonstrate how your service or product. This is most likely your one chance to convert a prospect into a customer, so carefully plan and prepare for this moment.

Demonstrating your product or service is the best way to convert a lead into a customer. When they see it, feel it, experience it, and hear it, it becomes experiential. Be excited and show your prospect why you are so passionate about your service or product, why they absolutely cannot live without it.

5. OVERCOME CUSTOMER OBJECTIONS

This is too expensive for me. I am not sure if I could use this product. I can do this myself for free. I am not looking to buy anything today. I just wanted some more information.

Objections are the roadblocks to your sale, and you need to gently knock them down, so they move forward toward purchasing your product or service. Objections come from fear or lack of excitement about your product. Most objections are the same, so use the chart below to practice your responses. It is human nature to find a reason to NOT buy something so be ready. So, not only do you need to combat and solve their hesitations, you need to also be flexible and ready to pivot.

6. GENERATE REFERRALS

The nanosecond the deal is done, you start working on the next one. Ask your customer (now buyer!) to refer friends and family to you. Follow up with your customer in a week to ensure they are happy with your product; give exceptional customer service every step of the way and they will come back to you over and over. Most products or services can be purchased anywhere, so the accessibility and service of the salesperson is more important than the actual product or service.

When you follow up with your buyer to see how they are doing with your service or product do not be shy about asking if they have any contacts, friends or family members that would be interested in the service or product. Ask for a referral. You can even start your own referral program and give your buyer points, a gift, or a discount for each referral they provide.

CHAPTER 21:

CONTRACTS: YOURS AND THEIRS!

CONTRACTS: THE ONES YOU SIGN

As an entrepreneur, you will be dealing with a lot of contracts. From leasing your office, your equipment, dealing with headhunters, vendors, contractors, independent contractors, sales contracts, and employee agreements, you need to follow one rule: **DO NOT SIGN ANYTHING UNTIL YOU HAVE READ IT ENTIRELY AND UNDERSTAND IT. Do not skip over words you do not understand, look them up, call your friends, and of course, consult your favorite lawyer.**

Different contracts are governed by different laws and every state has their own set of rules. But the basic construction is the same for each one.

If you do not understand what you are reading or how it affects your rights, have someone else read it for you. If you cannot afford a lawyer to review it, ask your smartest friend, and then ask another smart friend and so on. Never sign anything under duress or pressure.

On the other side of the coin, always get everything in writing, there is no such thing as a handshake agreement anymore. While some verbal agreements are still acceptable, when they are disputed it is literally a "he said/she said" situation and there are no guarantees as to who will win, even if one party is just being a dingdong and making trouble. There are no friends in business. Do not cut corners or make exceptions; business is business and stick to your guns on that.

ESSENTIAL ELEMENTS OF A BUSINESS CONTRACT

There are six required, essential elements for a contract to be valid. Valid just means that the contract can be enforced by the court.

All business contracts must have an Offer, an Acceptance, Consideration, and Mutual Consent. Then the contract must be signed by competent parties and the contract itself must be for a legal purpose. Let's translate that into real people's language.

1. **Offer:** The offer is what the contract promises will be given to the person who signs it. The offer should be as detailed as possible, and it needs to reflect what the parties discussed exactly. This is called "the meeting of the minds."

2. **Acceptance:** The acceptance is the written or verbal agreement to accept the offer exactly how written.

3. **Consideration:** Consideration is the most important part of a contract. Typically, it is one party's promise to pay money, but it can also be just a promise to perform (or not perform) an act. It is the bargained for exchange; something of value that is exchanged between the parties. Without consideration, a contract cannot exist.

4. **Mutual Consent:** Every contract must include a specific offer and acceptance of that specific offer. Both parties must consent to the terms using their own free will, of their own accord and without threat or pressure.

5. **Competent:** This means that parties are of "sound mind" to execute or enter a contract. This protects people such as those who are sick, mentally challenged, and older people with dementia from being taken advantage of. It also means that all parties are legal adults (over the age of eighteen or twenty-one, depending on the content of the offer). It also means that anyone who is on drugs at the time they execute the contract (legal or illegal if it makes your mind fuzzy, I'm not talking about Tylenol) so the contract will be considered "void" as if it never happened at all.

6. **Legal Purpose:** The contract must be for a legal purpose. You cannot enter a contract that would have criminal content, such as drugs or prostitution (yup).

WHEN A CONTRACT MUST BE IN WRITING

Some types of contracts are required to be in writing, or they are not considered legally valid. This a law known as the Statute of Frauds. Each state may vary a little, but some of the mist common types of contracts that must be in writing are:

1. Agreements that cannot be performed within a year of the date the contract was signed (such as a Rental Lease).

2. Contracts for the sale of goods that are in excess of $5000.

3. Real Estate Contracts that involve the sale or transfer of land.

4. Promises or agreements made in consideration of marriage (prenuptial agreement).

Now here is where things get tricky. Contracts can be "unilateral" or "bilateral." A unilateral contract means that only one party has an obligation. An example of a unilateral contract and insurance contract. The insurance company promises to pay the insured person a pre-determined amount of money if a pre-determined event happens. If the event does not happen, the company will not have to pay.

The good news is that most contracts are bilateral contracts which means both parties exchange promises to perform. One party's promise serves as consideration for the promise of the other.

Contract If you cannot have anyone review a contract for you, use this method to and chart to review your own contract.

CONTRACT REVIEW WORKSHEET

Industry:	
Who is executing the contract on the other side?	
What I know about them: (age, business reputation, active lawsuits, personal reputation, references)	
City State where other party is signing contract:	
My City and State:	
Term (length)	
Price and/or payments:	
Where payment is to be made:	
Is there interest on late payments?	
Is there a penalty for late payments?	
Contingencies: What I must do before signing:	
How the contingencies affect my business or life"	
Are the contingencies a hardship?	
What is the offer:	
How long do I have to accept the offer or make a counteroffer?	
I accept the offer as written:	Yes ___No____ write changes below
My counteroffer is:	
Is there an arbitration clause?	
What state is the jurisdiction for lawsuits?	
Am I responsible for attorney's fees if I lose?	
Is the state chosen for the jurisdiction of law suits a hardship for me?	
If I don't pay on time are their late fees and costs of collection?	
Does the contract automatically renew?	
How do I cancel the automatic renewal of this contract?	
Can this contract be assigned to someone else?	
How do I get out of this contract?	**See if your state requires a three-day cooling off period**
Did I sign everywhere as required?	
Did I initial everywhere as required?	
How do I deliver the signed acceptance or counteroffer of the contract?	

CONTRACTS: THE ONES YOU DRAFT

As a business owner you will need some basic contracts to start out. If you are selling a recurring product or service that will last over a year, you need a contract. If you are hiring employees, you need a contract. There are many websites where you can draft basic contracts for yourself and avoid the expense of an attorney, but I recommend if you are going to do all the leg work yourself, schedule a consultation with an attorney who can just look over what you have created to ensure compliance. If you plan on drafting and writing your own contracts to save money, educate yourself in the industry wide practices, look up versions from other similar companies and do your research.

Sales and/or Service Contracts

In order to stay compliant with state and local contract laws, any contract that extends over a year must be in writing to be valid. If you are providing any type of service, even if it includes physical or digital products, company provides professional services as opposed to selling a product, it needs to have its own good, standard form Services Contract (which can be labeled many things, including an Agreement for Professional Services). This type of agreement lays out the terms and conditions under which you provide services and specifically spells out your responsibilities and liabilities.

Having a good contract here is important. You want to avoid misunderstandings and undue liability. Ideally, this agreement gives you flexibility in completing the services, lists the fees for the job (and additional fees if you encounter unforeseen circumstances), and sets limitations on your liability (such as limiting that liability to the amount of the services fee).

Sales Contracts

Many businesses sell products, and therefore need a good Sales Contract. The Sales Contract lays out the price, terms, and conditions for the sale of goods, equipment, or other products. Of course, some businesses (like the corner grocery store) don't need Sales Contracts, but if your products sell for significant dollars, then you likely need a Sales Contract.

The actual Sales Contract can take the form of fine print on an order form or an invoice, or it can be tailor-made for a particular sale. You always want to start with your own form of contract. The key terms in Sales Contracts include price, price adjustments in certain events, responsibility for taxes, payment and credit terms, warranties to be given, disclaimers of various warranties, and liability limitations.

BASIC AGREEMENTS, CLAUSES AND DOCUMENTS FOR ENTREPRENEURS AND BUSINESSES

Founders' Agreement:

This contract outlines the roles, responsibilities, and ownership percentages of each founder. It may also cover issues like vesting schedules, decision-making processes, and dispute resolution mechanisms.

Employment Contract:

This is used when hiring employees. It outlines terms and conditions of employment, including roles, responsibilities, compensation, benefits, and termination clauses.

Independent Contractor Agreement:
When hiring freelancers or contractors, this agreement defines the scope of work, payment terms, deadlines, and any intellectual property rights associated with the work produced.

Non-Disclosure Agreement (NDA):
This contract is used to protect confidential information when sharing it with employees, contractors, or potential partners. It prevents them from disclosing or using sensitive information without permission.

Non-Compete Agreement:
This agreement restricts an employee or contractor from engaging in competing activities that could potentially harm the business. It specifies the duration and geographical scope of the non-compete clause.

Terms of Service/User Agreement (for online businesses):
This document sets out the rules and guidelines for using your website or platform. It covers issues like user conduct, content ownership, liability, and dispute resolution.

Privacy Policy (for online businesses):
This is a legal statement that informs users about how their personal information is collected, used, and protected by your business. It's especially important if your business collects any form of user data.

Sales Contract:
This outlines the terms of sale for your products or services, including pricing, payment terms, delivery, warranties, and any specific conditions.

Partnership Agreement (if applicable):
If you have business partners, this agreement outlines the terms and conditions of the partnership, including profit-sharing, decision-making, and dispute resolution procedures.

BASIC AGREEMENTS, CLAUSES, AND DOCUMENTS FOR AFFILIATE MARKETING

Affiliate marketing involves a partnership between a business (the advertiser) and individuals or other businesses (affiliates) who promote the advertiser's products or services in exchange for a commission on sales or other agreed-upon actions. To formalize this arrangement and protect the interests of both parties, several contracts are typically involved:

Affiliate Agreement
This is the central contract that outlines the terms and conditions of the affiliate program. It should cover key aspects such as commission structure, payment terms, promotional guidelines, reporting, and termination clauses.

Terms of Service (ToS)
This is a legal document that sets out the rules and guidelines for using the advertiser's website, products, or services. It may also include information about intellectual property rights, disclaimers, and limitations of liability.

Privacy Policy: This document outlines how the advertiser collects, uses, and protects personal information. It's important for compliance with privacy laws and to establish trust with customers.

Cookie Policy
If the affiliate program relies on tracking cookies to attribute sales, a cookie policy is crucial. It should explain how cookies are used, what information they collect, and how users can manage or disable them.

Compliance and Disclosure Agreement
This document ensures that affiliates adhere to relevant laws and regulations, including advertising and marketing standards, such as the Federal Trade Commission's (FTC) guidelines on disclosure.

Intellectual Property License Agreement
This outlines the rights and permissions granted to affiliates regarding the use of trademarks, logos, and other intellectual property owned by the advertiser. It sets boundaries on how affiliates can represent the brand.

Non-Disclosure Agreement (NDA)
In some cases, an NDA may be required to protect sensitive information that the advertiser shares with the affiliate, especially if it pertains to proprietary technology, upcoming products, or business strategies.

Termination Agreement
This states the circumstances under which the affiliate relationship can be terminated, as well as any associated penalties or consequences.

Dispute Resolution Clause
This specifies how any disputes or disagreements between the parties will be resolved, whether through arbitration, mediation, or litigation.

Governing Law and Jurisdiction
This clause identifies the legal jurisdiction and governing law that will apply to the contract. This is important in case any legal issues arise.

Liability Waiver and Indemnification
This clause outlines the responsibilities of each party in the event of legal claims or liabilities arising from the affiliate's actions.

Representations and Warranties
This section states the warranties and assurances made by each party, such as the affiliate's promise not to engage in deceptive marketing practices.

As you can see, there are so many different contracts, clauses, agreements, and terms that cross pollinate all areas of your business, so it is important to start with a solid foundation to build a house of bricks and stone, not a house of cards.

CHAPTER 22:

LAYING DOWN THE LAW

Entrepreneurs are usually focused on one thing: their idea and developing it into a successful business. The tedium of the day-to-day business tasks coupled with the mumbo jumbo of legal jargon can be the death of a great idea. In order to plant the seed that will grow into a successful crop, you must clear the land, plough the earth, till the dirt and know how to prevent and eradicate the pests that try to devour your crop. Those pests are the small mistakes that you can make unwittingly and the people that will attempt to exploit you for making them, so understanding some basic business law can help you with your pest control.

Even with a working knowledge of basic business law, without twenty years' experience as a business attorney, you need to know what you do not know. That means reaching out to a lawyer to review what you have come up with or having a lawyer prepare your contracts and business documents for you to ensure a healthy start to your business.

Start with these simple and broad categories to familiarize yourself with the areas where things can go wrong.

THE LAWS THAT GOVERN YOUR BUSINESS

No matter what industry you are in you need to fully understand the laws that govern your industry and your state of operation. You should also be aware that your state law may be stricter than the corresponding federal laws that will govern your business.

LICENSING

Determine if You Need a Business License

Some states and cities require occupational licenses or business licenses. You can determine this by going to the government website in your jurisdiction. Failure to obtain the appropriate license can result in fines or the closure of your business.

FEDERAL REGULATORY AGENCIES THAT REGULATE BUSINESSES

Governmental agencies play a crucial role in regulating businesses to ensure fair competition, protect consumers, and promote the overall well-being of the economy. Here are some of the key regulatory agencies in the United States:

Federal Trade Commission (FTC)

The FTC enforces antitrust laws and protects consumers from unfair or deceptive business practices. It monitors mergers and acquisitions to prevent monopolistic behavior and investigates and takes action against deceptive advertising and marketing practices.

Securities and Exchange Commission (SEC)

The SEC oversees the securities industry, which includes stocks, bonds, and other investment instruments. It enforces laws designed to ensure that markets are fair and transparent, and that investors are protected from fraud.

Environmental Protection Agency (EPA)

The EPA is responsible for enforcing environmental laws and regulations. It sets standards for air and water quality, oversees hazardous waste disposal, and regulates the use of chemicals and pesticides.

Occupational Safety and Health Administration (OSHA)

OSHA is responsible for setting and enforcing workplace safety and health standards. It conducts inspections, provides training, and enforces regulations to ensure safe working conditions.

Food and Drug Administration (FDA)

The FDA regulates the safety and effectiveness of food, drugs, medical devices, biologics, and other products. It reviews and approves new drugs and medical treatments and ensures the safety of the food supply.

Consumer Financial Protection Bureau (CFPB)

The CFPB supervises and enforces consumer protection laws related to financial products and services, such as mortgages, credit cards, and loans. It also educates consumers about their rights and responsibilities.

Federal Communications Commission (FCC)

The FCC regulates communication services, including radio, television, internet, and telecommunications. It ensures that these services are provided in a fair and competitive manner.

Department of Labor (DOL)

The DOL oversees various aspects of labor and employment, including wage and hour standards, workplace safety, unemployment insurance, and pension plans.

Department of Transportation (DOT)
The DOT regulates various aspects of transportation, including aviation, highways, railroads, and maritime. It sets safety and operational standards for transportation services.

Commodity Futures Trading Commission (CFTC)
The CFTC regulates the commodity futures and options markets. It oversees trading in commodities like agricultural products, energy, and financial instruments.

Department of Justice (DOJ
While not an independent regulatory agency, the DOJ plays a role in antitrust enforcement and prosecuting cases of corporate misconduct.

STATE AGENCIES THAT REGULATE BUSINESSES
State agencies that regulate businesses vary depending on the specific industry and the state in question and they also may have slightly different names.

Department of Commerce or Economic Development
These agencies often oversee a wide range of business-related activities, including business licenses, economic incentives, and workforce development programs.

Department of Revenue or Taxation
Responsible for administering and enforcing state tax laws, including sales tax, income tax, and business taxes.

Secretary of State
Handles business registration, including the filing of articles of incorporation, business names, and other legal documents.

Department of Labor
Regulates labor and employment laws, including minimum wage, workplace safety, and workers' compensation.

Department of Health or Health Services
Oversees businesses related to healthcare, including hospitals, clinics, and pharmacies.

Alcohol Beverage Control Board or Commission
Regulates the sale and distribution of alcoholic beverages, including licensing of bars, restaurants, and liquor stores.

Department of Agriculture or Food Safety
Regulates businesses involved in agriculture, food production, and food safety.

Department of Environmental Protection or Environmental Quality
Oversees businesses that may impact the environment, including manufacturing, waste management, and pollution control.

Department of Transportation
Regulates transportation-related businesses, including trucking companies, taxi services, and vehicle-related businesses.

Professional Licensing Boards
These boards oversee and regulate licensed professions such as doctors, lawyers, engineers, and other specialized fields.

Real Estate Commission
Regulates real estate agents and brokers, overseeing licensing and professional conduct.

Insurance Department
Regulates insurance companies, agents, and policies within the state.

Department of Consumer Affairs or Consumer Protection
Protects consumers from unfair or deceptive business practices and may oversee licensing for certain professions.

It's important for you to know that the specific agencies and their responsibilities can vary from state to state, and some states may have additional agencies or different names for similar departments. They all have one thing in common though: they will come after you for breaking any of their rules. You also need to be aware if your industry has any specialized regulatory bodies that oversee businesses in your industry. If you are starting a business or need information about specific regulations in your state, you really should consult with a lawyer that specializes in that industry, so they give you some guidelines and make sure your documents and business practices are tailored to keep you out of trouble.

EMPLOYMENT LAWS

Fair Labor Standards Act (FLSA)
This act regulates federal minimum wage, overtime rules, child labor bans, and record keeping requirements. You'll want to read through it to make sure you comply with the current regulations. You will need to ensure that you aren't misclassifying employees and make sure you have accurate job descriptions and job duties that clearly define whether the position is hourly, salary, exempt or nonexempt from overtime.

Federal Equal Employment Opportunity laws (EEO)

Before hiring employees, fully understand the laws that prohibit discrimination based on race, color, religion, sex, or national origin. These laws also provide protection for equal pay between men and women and people with disabilities.

Family and Medical Leave Act (FMLA)

If you have more than fifty employees, you need to understand how the FLMA works. If you have an employee who is pregnant or dealing with a medical condition, or has a family member with a medical condition, there are rules you must follow.

Occupational Safety and Health Act (OSHA)

This law guarantees employees a safe work environment, free from recognized health hazards. Certain industries have strict safety regulations, and you need to know if you are required to follow those rules. There are certain posters you may need to post in your office space as well.

Workers' compensation

Most states require employers to carry Worker's Compensation insurance. Check with your state's Department of Labor.

Right to Work or At-Will work doctrine

This means employers can fire an employee at any time for any reason unless it's an illegal one. Check your state to determine if you are an at-will state (most are!).

In addition to federal taxes, you'll likely have to pay state taxes as well. Use this website to research your state tax requirements.

Employee Taxes

When you plan to bring on an employee, it impacts your taxes. The amount of time an employee works for you will make a difference when it comes to taxes, so research the difference between a W-2 employee and a 1099 employee before making any hiring decisions.

ADVERTISING AND MARKETING LAWS

Truth in Advertising and Marketing

Be careful when you are drafting advertising o social media posts, Yu can never mislead the consumer or make statements that you cannot substantiate.

CAN-SPAM Act

The CAN-SPAM Act regulates all commercial emails. When sending emails, you have to be straight forward with the content, and you are required to tell recipients where your business is located and give them a way to opt-out of your email messages that is easy and clear.

Telemarking Sales Law

Most companies sell their products by cold calling, texting, and advertising online, you'll need to brush up on the FTC's telemarketing rule. Under this rule, businesses must ship products within 30 days, provide delivery notices if a product is delayed, and give refunds if an order can't be filled. You'll also want to check out the rules surrounding the Do Not Call Registry.

ONLINE BUSINESS LAWS

Some of the laws below may be duplicated form the other sections, but these are the laws and regulations sales tax for marketplace sellers and online stores is dependent on many factors; the great news is there are applications that have automated this process so you can be compliant. Alaska, Delaware, Montana New Hampshire, and Oregon do not have sales tax.

Sales tax nexus occurs when your business has some kind of connection to a state. All states have a slightly different definition of nexus, but most of the time states consider that a "physical presence" or "economic connection" creates nexus.

How to determine economic nexus:
Physical presence can mean several things, including:
- Having an office
- Having an employee
- Having a warehouse
- Having an affiliate
- Storing inventory
- Economic nexus: Making a certain number of sales in a state (either a certain dollar amount or a certain number of transactions) gives you an economic nexus.
- Temporarily doing physical business in a state for a limited amount of time, such as at a trade show.

State laws on economic nexus vary. The sales thresholds vary from $10,000 to $500,000 in sales, and some states do not have a transaction threshold at all. You must check each state you do business with if you do not have it automated through your e-commerce platform.

"Notice and report" laws are state laws that require online sellers with no physical presence in a state to either collect sales tax or provide a significant amount of reporting to states and their buyers if they meet a certain revenue or transaction threshold. While this sounds like economic nexus laws, they are slightly different.

STEPS FOR ECOMMERCE SALES TAX COMPLIANCE (ALSO DISCUSSED BELOW)

1. Register for a sales tax permit.
Register for a sales tax permit in your nexus state.

You do this by contacting your state's taxing authority (usually called the "[State] Department of Revenue.")

Most states consider it illegal to collect sales tax without a permit so you will need a valid sales tax permit before collecting.

Take note that the higher your sales volume in a state, the more often the state will want you to file a sales tax return and remit the sales tax you've collected.

2. Collect sales tax.
Start collecting sales tax online for all online shopping carts and marketplaces. Each shopping cart and marketplace will have a way to collect sales tax. There are two different ways to tax, and they are called Origin & Destination-Based Sales Tax Sourcing.

States are either "origin-based" or "destination-based" sales tax sourcing. You must check each state you are doing business with and the state in which you are operating.

That means that states get to decide whether online sellers charge sales tax based at the sales tax rate of their business location (origin-based sourcing), or whether online sellers are required to collect sales tax at the customer's ship to address (destination-based sourcing.)

Most states are destination-based. The purpose behind that is to ensure that every local area receives the exact amount of sales tax collected from buyers in their jurisdiction.

3. Report and File Sales Tax

When they issue your sales tax permit the state will assign sales tax filing frequency.

This means your sales tax due date will roll around either monthly, quarterly, or annually (and sometimes semi-annually.) Most states want to know how much sales tax you collected from buyers in each taxing jurisdiction.

You should consider Ecommerce Sales Tax Software to automate this process for you.

There has been some legal activity on this subject. On January 29, 2020, the Louisiana Supreme Court held that Walmart. com was not required to collect local sales tax on third-party sales facilitated through its online marketplace. The majority concluded Walmart.com was not a "dealer" under Louisiana law for purposes of sales and the company's contracts with third-party marketplace retailers did not transfer the third-party retailers' sales tax obligation to Walmart.com. What this means is that if you are a marketplace seller you are obligated and required to collect and pay the taxes.

Restore Online Shopper's Confidence Act (ROSCA).

If you are an e-commerce entrepreneur, then you need to know all about the Restore Online Shopper's Confidence Act (ROSCA). ROSCA prohibits any person from charging any consumer for goods or services sold in an Internet-based transaction through a negative option feature unless the person: It's essential to check for any updates or amendments to ROSCA as your businesses evolves. The Federal Trade Commission (FTC) is usually the primary enforcer of ROSCA, and they provide guidance and information about compliance with the law on their official website.

ROSCA requires that you provide text that clearly and conspicuously discloses all material terms of the transaction before obtaining the consumer's billing information. That means you have to show the customer if there is a shipping charge, the total of the shopping cart with a line for each item; basically, you can't sneak in an upgrade, subscription, or any added products, bundles, or VIP charge.

2. Obtains a consumer's express informed consent before obtaining the consumer's credit card, debit card, bank account, or other financial account for products or services sold through such transaction; and

3. Provides a simple mechanism for a consumer to stop recurring charges from being placed on the consumer's credit card, debit card, bank account, or other financial account.

The basics are disclosure, consent, confirmation, and cancellation.

1. **Disclosures:**
   a. Pricing plans / program offers (length of term, price).
   b. For trial offers: When the trial ends, the price that will be charged after the trial ends.
      pricing changes once the trial ends
   c. The subscription agreement will continue until the consumer cancels.

    d. The amount of recurring charges
    e. The length of the subscription term (e.g., monthly, annually, etc.)
    f. Minimum purchase obligation if any
    g. A description of the cancellation policy that applies to the offer

You also must:

    a. Disclose whether additional taxes or other fees apply to each payment
    b. Disclose amount of approximate taxes when known; until then reference applicable tax. Example: "$19.95 (+ applicable tax) per month"
    c. Disclose additional fees, when due, what they are for, etc. like shipping for free book.
    d. You must disclose if there is an early termination fee, if any; this is closely watched by the FTC, subject to litigation
    e. Disclosure of reactivation fee, if any.

Disclosures Must Be Made

In a "clear and conspicuous" manner before obtaining the consumer's billing information—in visual proximity or, in the case of an offer conveyed by voice, in temporal proximity to the request for consent to the offer.

Not buried only in long-form terms of service

Written disclosures (online or print): In a larger type than the surrounding text, or in contrasting type, font, or color to the surrounding text of the same size or set off from the surrounding text of the same size by symbols or other marks, in a manner that clearly calls attention to the language.

2. Consent

You must obtain the customer's affirmative, express informed consent before obtaining the consumer's credit card, debit card, bank account, or other financial account.

Express consent: Must be the affirmative/explicit agreement of the consumer to enroll.

Informed consent: Having been informed of the offer disclosures, the consumer provides informed consent.

A check box that consumers must affirmatively check to indicate the offer is preferred.

Example: "I accept" or "I agree" button may be acceptable, depending on disclosure placement and page layout.

3. Confirmation

The Federal Trade Commission (FTC) requires that merchants send an acknowledgment— "in a manner that is capable of being retained by the consumer"— that includes the offer terms, the cancellation policy, and information regarding how to cancel.

This can be the choice between:

- YES, along with my FREE book (plus shipping costs), I want the trial to Entrepreneur's Law Group for free, and I understand I will be charged $99 per month after my FREE trial is over.

- ○ NO, I do not want the FREE trial to the Entrepreneur's Law Group, but I would like to continue with my FREE book (plus shipping costs).

If the offer includes a gift or trial, you MUST disclose how to cancel and allow the consumer to cancel before the consumer pays for the "free" goods or services. The next page must provide information on how to cancel AND must disclose any shipping fees.

4. Cancellation

FTC standard for ROSCA Compliance
You must provide a simple mechanism for a consumer to stop recurring charges on their credit card, debit card, bank account, or other financial account. Recent FTC settlement orders clearly dictate that If the consumer enrolled online, then they must be able to cancel over the Internet or other web-based application.

Also, the biggest thing: You MUST show the total price in the shopping cart before the customer checks out. They have to see everything they have placed in their cart, and they have to have another chance to opt out and/or cancel.

INTELLECTUAL PROPERTY

Protect your intellectual property
You need a patent if you have developed an innovative or new product. You should also register for trademarks and service marks for your business name, symbols, and logos. You can do this by logging on to the United States Patent and Trademark Office and filling out the application.

If you have authored content such as a book or digital work, you can file for a copyright at the United States Copyright Office website.

Contract Law

There are options for you even if you cannot have a full-time in-house attorney. There are companies that provide monthly subscriptions for business consulting and inhouse counsel services. That is the service that my company provides.

At one point in the opening of your business, you should have at least one consultation with an attorney, accountant, human resource management professional and/or business consultant.

What Is a Contract?

Simply put, a contract is a legally enforceable document where the parties agree to do—or agree NOT to do—something. However, you cannot enter into a contract if it is for something illegal, such as a joint venture for a crime.

All enforceable contracts have the same elements.

1. **Offer:** First, the contract has to OFFER something.

2. **Acceptance:** The contract must have an acceptance of that offer. If the other party makes any changes to the offer that is called a counteroffer. A counteroffer is a rejection to the offer, hence no contract. Any counteroffer must be accepted.

3. **Intent**: The contract must clearly show the **intent** of both parties to enter into a legally binding agreement. In other

words, both parties must be aware that the agreement could be enforced by law.

4. **Consideration**: All contracts must have consideration. "Consideration" is usually money, but it could be anything of value.

The offer and the acceptance, then the consideration is the bargained for exchange for the product or service that is being offered. Such as, I offer to mow your lawn. If you accept, then you agree to pay me $20 per service. To show me you are serious, you pay for the first service ahead of time.

Another element to a valid contract is that all parties must be competent to enter into an agreement. That means the parties must be over the age of eighteen and of sound mind. They also must enter into the contract voluntarily without being bullied or forced.

Some agreements can be oral, but naturally their enforceability is stronger if they are written. If the agreement is oral, you must prove that the agreement happened and prove the terms. Some contracts, like those that cannot be performed in under a year, are required to be in writing. That is called the Statute of Frauds.

Always have solid contracts for your business actions. If you have a high value contract, you should always seek advice to ensure that you are protected.

There are options for you even if you cannot have a full-time in-house attorney. There are companies that provide monthly subscriptions for business consulting and inhouse counselling services.

At one point in the opening of your business, you should have at least one consultation with an attorney, accountant, human resource management professional and/or business consultant.

CHAPTER 23:

E-COMMERCE SALES TAX: *TO COLLECT OR NOT TO COLLECT...*

Taxes are flipping tricky. And tax issues are serious offenses if done incorrectly or not done at all. Do not set up anything yourself unless you are a tax professional or financial wizard. Even if you are, hire a third party to be at arms' length if something goes awry. Nothing in this chapter is tax advice or legal advice, just information to consider so you can have a meaningful conversation with your professionals.

To further complicate the process, every state is different and there is no uniformity at all to how states charge, determine, collect, and penalize tax liabilities on companies and corporations. However, there are five states (New Hampshire, Oregon, Montana, Alaska, and Delaware) do not impose any general, statewide sales tax, whether on goods or services. That is five less headaches.

TAX COMPLIANCE

There are a few steps to tax compliance that sum it up, but again, consult a tax professional as every situation is different. I suggest making yourself a digital spreadsheet and/or chart to refer to and ensure you are transacting on a platform that can keep track of your sales by states because all states use something called a nexus to determine if you have tax due in their state. Sales tax nexus occurs when your business has some kind of connection to a state. All states have a slightly different definition of nexus, but most of the time states consider that a "physical presence" or "economic connection" creates nexus. Simply put, if you have a brick and mortar space you are selling from, a warehouse, an employee, an affiliate, a storage space, and/or an office to effectuate making a sale you have a physical presence. If you sell over a certain sum, you have economic nexus and you are required to pay taxes. So here is the play:

1. Keep track of your sales by state.
2. Keep track of your sales by tangible products, intangible products (digital books and assets) and by services (consulting, personal and/or educational training).
3. List the states that you have sold in and how much your gross sales are in that state.
4. Determine what states with which you have met the threshold for establishing a sales tax nexus.
5. Determine which of your products are subject to sales tax.
6. Register for a sales tax permit in the states where you have met the threshold to pay tax.
7. Set up automatic sales tax collection on your online shopping carts and marketplaces.
8. Accurately report how much sales tax you collected.
9. Always timely file your sales tax returns.

There are goods and services and there are brick and mortar and e-commerce. There are combinations of all the above; so, sketch out your business structure first. Make a list of your services and goods. Make a list of the states where you will make sales, provide services or digital products. If you can automate it, do it.

ECOMMERCE SALES
States that Charge for Digital Products

State	Taxable	Note
Alabama	YES	Digital downloads are generally considered tangible personal property and are taxable at the same rate as other tangible personal property.
Alaska	NO	No sales tax in the state.
Arizona	YES	Digital downloads are generally considered tangible personal property and are subject to gross receipts tax.
Arkansas	NO	Digital subscriptions are also tax exempt. Changing to taxable in 2018.
California	NO	If you provide a physical copy or physical storage, then the sale is taxable.
Colorado	YES	Electronic delivery of "legal publication" newspapers are exempt since physical copies of those same newspapers are exempt.
Connecticut	YES	Sales or purchases of 'digital downloads' from the Internet are taxed at a reduced rate of 1%.
Delaware	NO	No sales tax in the state.
Florida	NO	If the item is sold with tangible personal property, then the entire sale would most likely be subject to Florida sales tax.
Georgia	NO	No sales tax in the state.
Hawaii	YES	Digital products are taxable in Hawaii.
Idaho	YES	Taxable if permanent right to use, Tax-exempt if leasing or renting the product.
Illinois	NO	Digital products are tax exempt in Illinois.
Indiana	YES	Includes audio works, audio visual works and books.
Iowa	YES	Digital products and services related to them
Kansas	NO	No sales tax in the state.
Kentucky	YES	Considered tangible personal property.

Louisiana	YES	Digital products are taxable in Louisiana.
Maine	YES	Digital products are taxable in Maine.
Maryland	NO	Maryland does not expressly state whether digital products are taxable or non-taxable, so it is generally assumed they are tax exempt.
Massachusetts	NO	No sales tax in the state.
Michigan	NO	No sales tax in the state.
Minnesota	YES	Considered tangible personal property. Student digital textbooks and instructional materials are exempt.
Mississippi	YES	Digital products are taxable in Mississippi.
Missouri	NO	No sales tax in the state.
Montana	NO	No sales tax in the state.
Nebraska	YES	Digital products and digital codes to access such products are also taxable.
Nevada	NO	Also includes audio-visual works, for both temporary and permanent sales.
New Hampshire	NO	No sales tax in the state.
New Jersey	YES	Includes digital audio-visual works like movies, audio works like music and ringtones and digital books.
New Mexico	YES	Digital products are taxable in New Mexico. Most transactions are subject to New Mexico's gross receipts tax (the state's version of sales tax).
New York	NO	However, there are some exceptions to eBooks.
North Carolina	YES	Digital audio works, audiovisual works, books, magazines, newspapers, newsletters, reports or other publications, photographs or greeting cards delivered electronically are all considered tangible personal property.

North Dakota	NO	No sales tax in the state.
Ohio	YES	Digital audiovisual work, digital audio work and digital books are taxable.
Oklahoma	NO	No sales tax in the state.
Oregon	NO	No sales tax in the state.
Pennsylvania	YES	Photos, books, games, and other downloads are taxable.
Rhode Island	NO	No sales tax in the state.
South Carolina	NO	No sales tax in the state.
South Dakota	YES	Digital products are tax exempt in South Carolina.
Tennessee	YES	Digital products are tax exempt in Tennessee.
Texas	YES	Taxable as long as the item also taxable if sold in physical format.
Utah	YES	Digital products are taxable in Utah.
Vermont	YES	Digital products are taxable in Vermont, whether transferred electronically for permanent or temporary use.
Virginia	NO	No sales tax in the state.
Washington	YES	Digital products are taxable in Washington. This includes downloaded digital goods like music and movies, streamed and accessed digital goods, and digital automated services.
Washington DC	YES	Digital products include audio/audiovisual works, e-books, digital codes, apps, games, and any other taxable tangible personal property that's digitally delivered, streamed, or accessed, purchased singly or by subscription.
West Virginia	NO	No sales tax in the state.
Wisconsin	YES	Digital goods are taxable in Wisconsin. This includes audio works, audiovisual works, books, and codes used to purchase works (digital or physical) by digital means.
Wyoming	YES	Digital products are taxable in Wyoming. This includes digital audio works, audio visual works and books.

Now it gets a little tricky because some states charge tax on consulting services. There are four states that tax services by default, which are Hawaii, South Dakota, New Mexico, and West Virginia, but with exceptions only for services specifically exempted in the law. In the rest of the forty-one states and the District of Columbia, services are not taxed by default, but services specified by the state may be taxed. Now to add yet another layer of confusion, consulting services can also be deemed as income and may be taxed as self-employment income, so independent consultants may have to pay both income tax and self-employment tax.

Hawaii, New Mexico, South Dakota, West Virginia, and Washington tax consulting services; some by default and some by specification.

Economic Nexus and Threshold Amounts

For my fellow Floridians, Florida has no economic nexus laws, but legislation is constantly evolving, with new states being added frequently. State laws on economic nexus vary. The sales thresholds vary from $10,000 to $500,000 in sales, and some states do not have a transaction threshold at all.

There are also "Notice and report" state laws that require online sellers with no physical presence in a state to either collect sales tax or provide a significant amount of reporting to states and their buyers if they meet a certain revenue or transaction threshold. While this sounds like economic nexus laws, they are slightly different.

THRESHOLD AMOUNTS BY STATE

Alabama
Threshold: $250,000/year based on the previous calendar year's sales

Snapshot: According to state law, sellers who exceed the $250,000 sales threshold are required to register for an Alabama sales tax permit, collect sales tax on sales that ship to Alabama, and remit that sales tax to the state.

Arizona
Threshold: In 2020, the threshold will be $150,000, and then $100,000 in 2021 and thereafter.

Snapshot: According to state law, sellers who exceed the gross sales OR transaction number are required to register for an Arizona sales tax permit to collect transaction privilege tax (TPT) on sales that ship to Arizona and remit the sales tax to the state.

Arkansas
Threshold: $100,000/year in gross revenue or two hundred or more separate transactions on the previous calendar year's sales

Snapshot: According to state law, sellers who exceed the gross sales OR transaction number are required to register for an Arkansas sales tax permit, collect sales tax on sales that ship to Arkansas, and remit the sales tax to the state.

California
Threshold: $500,000/year in gross revenue on the previous or current calendar year's sales

Snapshot: According to state law, remote sellers in California who exceed the $500K gross sales are required to register with the CDTFA, collect sales tax on sales that ship to California, and remit the sales tax to the state.

Colorado
Threshold: $100,000/year in gross revenue on the previous or current calendar year's sales

Snapshot: According to state law, sellers who exceed the gross sales are required to register for a_Colorado sales tax permit, collect sales tax on sales that ship to Colorado, and remit the sales tax to the state.

Connecticut
Threshold: $100,000 in gross receipts during the 12-month period;/ year in gross revenue AND 200 or more separate transactions on the previous calendar year's sales.

Snapshot: According to state law, sellers who exceed the gross sales AND transaction number are required to register for a Connecticut sales tax permit, collect sales tax on sales that ship to Connecticut, and remit the sales tax to the state.

Georgia
Threshold: $100,000/year in gross revenue, or makes sales into Georgia in more than two hundred separate transactions in the previous or current calendar year

Snapshot: According to the state, sellers that meet either the sales or transaction number thresholds are required to register for a Georgia sales tax permit, collect sales tax on sales that ship into Georgia, and remit sales tax to the state.

Hawaii
Threshold: $100,000/year in gross revenue, or makes sales into Hawaii in more than two hundred separate transactions in the previous or current calendar year

Snapshot: According to the state, sellers that meet either the sales or transaction number thresholds are required to register for a Hawaii sales tax permit, collect sales tax on sales that ship into Hawaii, and remit sales tax to the state.

Idaho

Threshold: $100,000 of sales made in Idaho in the previous or current calendar year.

Snapshot: According to the state, sellers that meet either the sales or transaction number thresholds are required to register for an Idaho sales tax permit, collect sales tax on sales that ship into Hawaii, and remit sales tax to the state.

Illinois

Threshold: $100,000/year in gross revenue, or makes sales into Illinois in more than two hundred separate transactions in the previous twelve months

Snapshot: According to the state, sellers that meet either the sales or transaction number thresholds are required to register for an Illinois sales tax permit, collect sales tax on sales that ship into Illinois, and remit sales tax to the state.

Indiana

Threshold: $100,000 in gross revenue in the previous calendar year, or makes sales into Indiana in more than two hundred separate transactions in the current or last calendar year

Snapshot: According to state law, sellers who exceed either the gross sales or transaction number threshold are required to register for an Indiana sales tax permit, collect sales tax on sales that ship to Indiana, and remit that sales tax to the state.

Iowa

Threshold: $100,000/year in gross revenue in the previous or current calendar year.

Snapshot: According to the state, sellers that meet the sales thresholds are required to register for an Iowa sales tax permit, collect sales tax on sales that ship into Iowa, and remit sales tax to the state. For those under the threshold, it is voluntary, but you can register for an Iowa Retailer's Use Tax (RUT) permit, although not required.

Kansas

Threshold: There is no exception for small sellers, so all remote sellers with sales in Kansas will meet economic nexus. It is worth noting however, that there is a conflicting opinion from the Attorney General due to the unique nature of this legislation, so sellers will want to monitor this threshold law closely in order to see if it lifts to a higher requirement or is overturned. As it stands now, the Department of Revenue is still requiring out-of-state sellers to remit sales tax.

Snapshot: According to state law, all sellers who make sales in Kansas must register for a Kansas sales tax permit regardless of sales or transactions.

Kentucky

Threshold: $100,000/year in gross revenue, or makes sales into Kentucky in more than two hundred separate transactions in the previous or current calendar year

Snapshot: According to the state, sellers that meet either the sales or transaction number thresholds are required to register for a Kentucky sales tax permit, collect sales tax on sales that ship into Kentucky, and remit sales tax to the state.

Louisiana
Threshold: $100,000/year in gross revenue, or makes sales into Louisiana in more than two hundred separate transactions in the previous or current calendar year

Snapshot: According to the state, sellers that meet either the sales or transaction number thresholds are required to register for a Louisiana sales tax permit, collect sales tax on sales that ship into Louisiana, and remit sales tax to the state.

Maine
Threshold: $100,000 in gross revenue in the previous calendar year or current calendar year, or makes sales into Maine in more than two hundred separate transactions in the previous calendar year or current calendar year

Snapshot: According to state law, sellers who either exceed the gross sales or transaction number threshold are required to register for a Maine sales tax permit, collect sales tax on sales shipped to Maine, and remit that sales tax to the state.

Maryland
Threshold: $100,000/year in gross revenue or makes sales into Maryland in more than two hundred separate transactions in the previous or current calendar year.

Snapshot: According to the state, sellers that meet either the sales or transaction number thresholds are required to register for a Maryland sales tax permit, collect sales tax on sales that ship into Maryland, and remit sales tax to the state.

Massachusetts
Threshold: $100,000 in sales over the preceding calendar year. The existing cookie nexus is $500,000 and one hundred transactions in the current or prior year.

Snapshot: According to state law, sellers who exceed the gross sales threshold are required to register for a Massachusetts sales tax permit, collect sales tax on sales that ship to Massachusetts, and remit that sales tax to the state.

Michigan
Threshold: $100,000 in gross revenue in the last calendar year or makes sales into Michigan in more than two hundred separate transactions in the previous calendar year.

Snapshot: According to state law, sellers who exceed the $100,000 threshold or the transaction number threshold are required to register for a Michigan sales tax permit, collect sales tax on sales that ship to Michigan, and remit sales tax to the state.

Minnesota
Threshold: $100,000 in gross revenue in the last 12 months or makes sales into Minnesota in more than two hundred separate transactions in the previous 12 months.

Snapshot: According to state law, sellers who exceed either the $100,000 threshold or the transaction number threshold are required to register for a Minnesota sales tax permit, collect sales tax on sales that ship to Minnesota, and remit sales tax to the state.

Mississippi

Threshold: Sales into Mississippi that exceed $250,000 in the prior twelve months

Snapshot: According to state law, sellers who exceed the $250,000 threshold are required to register for a Mississippi sales tax permit, collect sales tax on sales that ship to Mississippi, and remit sales tax to the state.

Nebraska

Threshold: Sales into Nebraska exceeding $100,000 or sales were made in two hundred or more separate transactions in the current or last calendar year.

Snapshot: According to the state, sellers who exceed the sales threshold or transaction number are required to register for a Nebraska sales tax permit, collect sales tax on sales that ship into Nebraska, and remit sales tax to the state.

Nevada

Threshold: $100,000/year in gross revenue the previous calendar year OR 200 or more separate transactions in the previous or current calendar year.

Snapshot: According to the state, sellers that meet either the sales or transaction number thresholds are required to register for a Nevada sales tax permit, collect sales tax on sales that ship into Nevada, and remit sales tax to the state.

New Jersey

Threshold: Sales of $100,000 in New Jersey, or more than two hundred transactions in the state in the current or last calendar year.

Snapshot: According to the state, sellers that meet either the sales or transaction number thresholds are required to register for a New Jersey sales tax permit, collect sales tax on sales that ship into New Jersey, and remit sales tax to the state.

New Mexico

Threshold: $100,000 in annual gross revenue from sales in New Mexico in the last calendar year.

Snapshot: According to the state, remote sellers and marketplace facilitators are required to register, collect, and remit gross receipts tax to the state if they meet the sales thresholds

New York

Threshold: $500,000 per year in gross revenue AND sales made in New York in more than one hundred separate transactions in the last four quarters.

Snapshot: According to the state, sellers that meet both the sales and transaction number thresholds are required to register for a New York sales tax permit, collect sales tax on sales that ship into New York, and remit sales tax to the state. The increase from the prior threshold of $300,000 for businesses that have no physical presence in New York is **effective retroactively to June 21, 2018**. The increase for marketplace providers is effective retroactively to June 1, 2019.

North Carolina

Threshold: $100,000/year in gross revenue or makes sales into North Carolina in more than two hundred separate transactions in the current or last calendar year.

Snapshot: According to the state, sellers that meet either the sales or transaction number thresholds are required to register for a North Carolina sales tax permit, collect sales tax on sales that ship into North Carolina, and remit sales tax to the state.

North Dakota

Threshold: Sales into North Dakota exceeding $100,000 in the current or last calendar year.

Snapshot: According to the state, sellers who exceed the sales threshold are required to register for a North Dakota sales tax permit, collect sales tax on sales that ship into North Dakota, and remit sales tax to the state.

SMALL SELLER EXCEPTION: North Dakota law includes an exception for small sellers which will require sales tax collection by remote sellers ONLY IF their taxable sales into the state exceed $100,000 in the current or previous calendar year.

Ohio

Threshold: Sales of $100,000 or more annually or two hundred or more separate transactions into the state in the current or last calendar year.

Snapshot: According to the state, sellers that meet either the sales or transaction number thresholds are required to register for an Ohio sales tax permit, collect sales tax on sales that ship into Ohio, and remit sales tax to the state.

Oklahoma

Important note: This is a "notice & report law" which was not affected by the *South Dakota v. Wayfair* case. That means that this law has been in effect and was being legally enforced before the June 2018 ,21, date the *Wayfair* ruling was handed down.

Threshold: Sales in Oklahoma of at least $100,000 in the previous 12 months.

Sellers who meet the threshold are required to elect to do one of the following on or before June 1 of each calendar year:

1. Register for an Oklahoma sales tax permit and collect sales tax on Oklahoma sales.
2. Comply with Oklahoma's notice and reporting requirements.

Pennsylvania

Important note: Prior to January 2019, Pennsylvania's law was a "notice & report law" which was not affected by the *South Dakota v. Wayfair* case. That means that this law has been in effect and was being legally enforced before the June 21, 2018, date the *Wayfair* ruling was handed down. You can read more about notice & report laws here. For those who meet the new thresholds below, there are additional guidelines in effect.

Threshold: Sales into Pennsylvania that exceeded $100,000 in the previous 12-month period are considered to have an economic nexus. The notice and report are still in effect for those with taxable sales greater than $10,000 but less than $100,000 in a calendar year.

Snapshot: According to Pennsylvania, sellers who meet the nexus threshold are required to register for a Pennsylvania sales tax permit, collect sales tax on sales that ship into Pennsylvania, and remit sales tax to the state.

Those who do not meet the economic threshold should make an election by March 1 of every year and do one of two things:

1. Register for a Pennsylvania sales tax permit, collect sales tax on sales that ship into Pennsylvania, and remit sales tax to the state.
2. Comply with the state's rigorous "notice and reporting requirements."

Rhode Island

Prior to July 1, 2019, Rhode Island enacted a "notice & report law" for non-collecting sellers which was not affected by the *South Dakota v. Wayfair* case. That means that this law has been in effect and was being legally enforced before the June 2018, 21, date the *Wayfair* ruling was handed down. Remote sellers in Rhode Island were required to collect and remit sales tax *or* comply with non-collecting seller use tax notice and reporting requirements. After July 2019, 1, remote sellers will be obligated to register for a sales tax permit in Rhode Island if they exceed the below thresholds.

Threshold: Sales in Rhode Island that exceed $100,000 or more, or two hundred separate transactions in the state in a calendar year.

Snapshot: According to the state, sellers that meet either the sales or transaction number thresholds are required to register for a Rhode Island sales tax permit, collect sales tax on sales that ship into Rhode Island, and remit sales tax to the state.

It is worth noting that Rhode Island is not repealing, nor eliminating the use tax notice and reporting requirements for non-collecting sellers. Remote sellers who meet the thresholds no longer have the option to comply with the existing use tax notice and report; however, remote sellers who do not satisfy the economic nexus threshold have the choice to register to collect sales tax in Rhode Island *or* comply with the notice and report for non-collecting sellers.

South Carolina
Threshold: Sales of $100,000 in South Carolina in the previous or current calendar year

Snapshot: According to the state, sellers that meet either the sales or transaction number thresholds are required to register for a South Carolina sales tax permit, collect sales tax on sales that ship into South Carolina, and remit sales tax to the state.

South Dakota
Threshold: Sales of $100,000 in South Dakota, or more than two hundred transactions in the state in the current or last calendar year

Snapshot: According to the state, sellers that meet either the sales or transaction number thresholds are required to register for a South Dakota sales tax permit, collect sales tax on sales that ship into South Dakota, and remit sales tax to the state.

Tennessee
Threshold: Sales exceeding $500,000 in the state in the previous 12 months

Snapshot: According to the state, sellers with sales exceeding the threshold are required to register for a Tennessee sales tax permit, collect sales tax on sales that ship into Tennessee, and remit sales tax back to the state.

Texas

Threshold: Sales above $500,000 in Texas in the previous calendar year.

Snapshot: Remote sellers with Texas revenues above $500,000 are required to register for a sales tax permit, collect sales tax on sales that ship to Texas, and remit the sales tax to the state. Remote sellers with Texas revenue below this amount will not have to register and collect tax.

Utah

Threshold: Sales of $100,000 or more in the state, or at least two hundred individual sales transactions into the state in the current or last calendar year.

Snapshot: According to the state, sellers with sales equal to or exceeding the sales or transaction number thresholds are required to register for a Utah sales tax permit, collect sales tax on sales that ship into Utah, and remit sales tax to the state.

Vermont

Threshold: Sales of $100,000 or more in the state, or at least two hundred individual sales transactions in the state during any preceding twelve-month period.

Snapshot: According to the state, sellers with sales equal to or exceeding the sales or transaction number thresholds are required to register for a Vermont sales tax permit, collect sales tax on sales that ship into Vermont, and remit sales tax to the state.

Virginia

Threshold: Sales of $100,000 or more in Virginia, or at least two hundred individual sales transactions into the state if in the previous or current calendar year.

Snapshot: According to the state, sellers with sales equal to or exceeding the sales or transaction number thresholds are required to register for a Virginia sales tax permit, collect sales tax on sales that ship into Virginia, and remit sales tax to the state. Register online or complete Form R-1.

Washington

Economic Nexus Threshold: Sales of $100,000 or more into the state into Washington in the current or last calendar year.

According to the state, sellers with sales equal to or exceeding the sales number thresholds are required to register for a Washington sales tax permit, collect sales tax on sales that ship into Washington, and remit sales tax to the state.

Prior to March 14, 2019, remote sellers could also have economic nexus if they had two hundred or more transactions in the state. And, effective as of July 1, 2019, a new bill eliminated both the notice and reporting requirements established in the state's 2018 Marketplace Fairness law in addition to the 200-transaction trigger. If you previously registered because you met the 200-transaction threshold, have your accounting or finance professional; assess your sales to see if you exceed the $100,000. If you do, you must continue to collect and submit retail sales tax.

Washington DC

Threshold: Sales of $100,000 in Washington D.C. or more than two hundred transactions in the state in the previous calendar year.

Snapshot: According to state law, remote sellers in Washington D.C. who exceed the $100K gross sales or the two hundred transactions number are required to register, collect sales tax on sales that ship to Washington D.C., and remit the sales tax to the state.

West Virginia

Threshold: Sales of $100,000/year in gross revenue the previous calendar year OR 200 or more separate transactions in the previous or current calendar year.

Snapshot: According to the state, sellers that meet either the sales or transaction number thresholds are required to register for a West Virginia sales tax permit, collect sales tax on sales that ship into West Virginia, and remit sales tax to the state.

Wisconsin

Threshold: Sales of $100,000 or more annually or two hundred or more separate transactions into the state in the current or last calendar year.

Snapshot: Unlike other states on this list, Wisconsin did not have an economic nexus law in effect before *Wayfair v. South Dakota*. However, in response to the SCOTUS decision, the Wisconsin Department of Revenue issued a statement about how Wisconsin intends to enforce the Wayfair decision.

Wyoming

Threshold: Sales of $100,000 or more into the state, or two hundred or more separate transactions into the state in the current or last calendar year.

Snapshot: According to the state, sellers with sales equal to or exceeding the sales or transaction number thresholds are required to register for a Wyoming sales tax permit, collect sales tax on sales that ship into Wyoming, and remit sales tax to the state.

STEPS FOR ECOMMERCE COMPLIANCE

Register for a sales tax permit.
Register for a sales tax permit in your nexus state.

You do this by contacting your state's taxing authority (usually called the "[State] Department of Revenue.") The state will require identifying information from about the business and business activities (what we sell).

Most states consider it illegal to collect sales tax without a permit, so we need a valid sales tax permit before collecting.

As a rule of thumb, the higher your sales volume in a state, the more often the state will want you to file a sales tax return and remit the sales tax you have collected.

Collect sales tax.
Start collecting sales tax online for all our online shopping carts and marketplaces. Each shopping cart and marketplace will have a way to collect sales tax. There are two different ways of tax, and they are called Origin & Destination-Based Sales Tax Sourcing.

States are either "origin-based" or "destination-based" sales tax sourcing.

That means that states get to decide whether online sellers charge sales tax based at the sales tax rate of their business location (origin-based sourcing), or whether online sellers are required to collect sales tax at the customer's ship to address (destination-based sourcing.)

Most states are destination-based. The purpose behind that is to ensure that every local area receives the exact amount of sales tax collected from buyers in their jurisdiction.

Report and File Sales Tax
When they issue our sales tax permit, the state assigns a sales tax filing frequency.

This means our sales tax due date will roll around either monthly, quarterly, or annually (and sometimes semi-annually.) most states want to know how much sales tax you collected from buyers in each taxing jurisdiction.

On January 29, 2020, the Louisiana Supreme Court issued a 4-3 decision in *Normand v. Wal-Mart.com USA,* reversing in full two lower courts and holding Walmart.com was not required to collect local sales tax on third-party sales facilitated through its online marketplace. The majority concluded Walmart.com was not a «dealer» under Louisiana law for purposes of such sales and the company›s contracts with third-party marketplace retailers did not transfer the third-party retailers› sales tax obligation to Walmart.com.

While dozens of states have enacted marketplace facilitator laws post-*Wayfair* requiring facilitators to collect sales tax on third-party marketplace sales, the Court's decision stands to have a broad impact in defining the role of marketplace facilitators particularly in the absence or prior to the adoption of such laws. What this means is that you are obligated and required to collect and pay the taxes.

As such, if you have an e-commerce store on a marketplace like Amazon or Walmart, you need a disclaimer that you understand that you will be collecting the sales tax. See the Chapter on Disclaimers and Disclosures for some sample language.

CHAPTER 24:

PRIVACY POLICY AND TERMS OF USE

THE PRIVACY POLICY

If you are collecting any data from consumers who visit your website or if you are an e-commerce business, then Privacy Policies are legally Required. Even if you are not required to have them, I would suggest you do it anyway, just in case you change the process later, so you are ready. If you are not collecting data, YOU SHOULD BE! The best digital marketing strategies all involve data collection. Privacy laws are not just applicable in the United States but are mandated around the world to any business collecting personal information from its website. The only way to prevent violating global and local laws is to have a privacy policy clearly posted to your site and available with your mobile application (app) if you have one.

What is a privacy policy, exactly? A privacy policy is a legal agreement that discloses to the consumers the type of personal information you collect, how you use this information, and how you keep it safe.

But consider this: the internet has a global reach, so you need to worry about the customers in Italy, Canada, and Australia as much as the customers in Arkansas, Utah, and Guam. Of course, California has even stricter laws, and then the kicker is that they all have different laws.

Examples of personal information are:

- Names
- Dates of birth
- Email addresses
- Physical addresses
- Personal details about height and weight
- Billing address
- Shipping addresses
- Phone numbers
- Bank information
- Social security numbers

A privacy policy covers:

- The use of cookies
- What type of information is collected by the website or app
- The purpose for such data collection
- Data storage, security, and access

PRIVACY LAWS IN THE EUROPEAN UNION (EU)

There are twenty-seven countries in the European Union. They are Austria, Italy, Belgium, Latvia, Bulgaria, Lithuania, Croatia, Luxembourg, Cyprus, Malta, Czechia, Netherlands, Denmark, Poland, Estonia, Portugal Finland, Romania, France, Slovakia, Germany, Slovenia, Greece, Spain, Hungary, Sweden, and Ireland. These countries all follow the General Data Protection Regulation

(GDPR). The GDPR was updated on May 25, 2018, and is stricter than the 1995 version.

The GDPR dictates that all companies operating in the EU, as well as foreign companies that handle personal data of people located in the EU, must have a privacy policy. It applies to both EU businesses as well as any international business that collects personal data from users located within the EU. If you have any type of ecommerce business, or if you are employing any digital marketing strategies you will need a privacy policy as you will be collecting data of people in the EU.

To be GDPR compliant you need to do the following:

Obtain clear consent: Consent must be easily given and freely withdrawn at any time.

1. **Communicate Timely breach notification:** You only have 72 hours to report data breached to both your customers and any data controllers, if your company is large enough to require a GDPR data controller. Failure to report breaches will result in fines.

2. **Right to data access:** If a consumer requests their existing data profile, you must be able to serve them with a fully detailed and free electronic copy of the data you have collected about them. This report must also include every single way you have been using their information.

3. **Data Deletion:** Consumers have the right to request that you totally erase their personal data.

4. **Data Portability:** Consumers must be able to obtain their data from you and reuse that data anywhere they want.

5. **Privacy by design:** This section of GDPR requires companies to design their systems with the proper security protocols in place from the start. Failure to design your systems of data collection the right way will result in a fine.

6. **Potential Data Protection Officers:** In some cases, your company may need to appoint a data protection officer (DPO) if your company is large enough and depending on how much data you collect.

PRIVACY LAWS IN CANADA

Canada's Personal Information Protection and Electronic Documents Act (PIPEDA) protects personal data belonging to Canadian citizens and requires companies operating online in Canada to have a privacy policy.

PIPEDA dictates the way that private-sector companies can collect, use, and disclose personal information for commercial purposes. It also applies to the personal information of employees of federally regulated businesses such as banks, airlines, and telecommunications companies. Governmental agencies follow a different set of laws just called Privacy Laws.

The 10 Privacy Principles of PIPEDA, also known as the *10 Fair Information Principles*, come from a national standard called the *CSA Model Code for the Protection of Personal Information*.

Accountability: You must designate someone to be accountable for data collection and management of personal information. You can choose someone internally and train them, it does not have to be a separate position.

Identifying Purposes: You must clearly identify the purposes for which personal information is collected, either before or at the time of collection.

1. Consent: You must have what they call "meaningful" consent. That means people must understand what they are consenting to. It is only considered valid if it is reasonable to expect that your customers will understand the nature, purpose, and consequences of the collection, use or disclosure of their personal information.

2. Limiting Collection: You must limit the collection of personal information to only what your organization needs to fulfill a legitimate identified purpose.

3. Limiting Use, Disclosure, and Retention: Your organization may use or disclose personal information only for the identified purposes for which it was collected. Keep personal information only as long as it is needed to serve those purposes and then delete it. You are required to know what personal information you have, where it is, and what you are doing with it. If you are going to use the information for a new purpose, you need to get "fresh" consent. You are required to have procedures in place for retaining and destroying personal information.

4. Accuracy: You are required to ensure that the information you have is accurate and that you are disclosing the information to any third parties.

5. Safeguards: You are required to protect all information with respect to how private or sensitive it is and always safeguard against loss, theft, and any unauthorized access.

6. Openness: Your privacy policy really needs to make sense, the consumer should understand why you collect data, how you protect data, how they can access and manage their data and how they can request for its deletion.

7. Individual Access: Consumers have the right to access their personal information. They also have the right to challenge accuracy, and have it amended if it is inaccurate.

8. Challenging Compliance: An individual must be able to challenge your organization's compliance with the fair information principles. They should address their challenge to the person in your organization who is accountable for compliance with PIPEDA.

PRIVACY LAWS IN AUSTRALIA

Privacy laws in Australia are covered by the Australian Privacy Act of 1988. This act mandates that all businesses collecting personal information online in Australia must have a privacy policy. There are thirteen Australian privacy principles that cover the collection, use and disclosure of personal information; an organization or agency's governance and accountability of how data is collected and used; how the data is protected; how the veracity of the data is maintained; and the rights of individuals to access their personal information. What is most interesting is that Australia has drafted these laws to be very neutral as far as technology, so they are easily adaptable when technology changes. So, when you are reading these, do not misinterpret that these apply to all methods of digital marketing even if it does not clearly state that. Not following the privacy laws if you are doing business in Australia is deemed an "interference with the privacy of an individual" which will land you involvement in a regulatory action and penalties Down Under.

Accordingly, APP entities must be aware of the full scope of the obligations imposed upon them according to the nature of their business activities.

The Australian Privacy Principles (APP)
APP 1: Open and transparent management of personal information
APP 2: Anonymity and pseudonymity
APP 3: Collection of solicited personal information
APP 4: Dealing with unsolicited personal information
APP 5: Notification of the collection of personal information
APP 6: Use or disclosure of personal information
APP 7: Direct marketing
APP 8: Cross-border disclosure of personal information
APP 9: Adoption, use or disclosure of government related identifiers
APP 10: Quality of personal information
APP 11: Security of personal information
APP 12: Access to personal information
APP 13: Correction of personal information

EXTRA-TERRITORIAL APPLICATION OF THE PRIVACY ACT

If you are an entity operating outside Australia you will still have to follow this Act if you have *'an Australian link'*, which is defined as any entity that was formed in Australia, has its central management and control in Australia, or is conducting business and collects or holds a consumer's personal information in Australia. So, this means that overseas entities, or any such Australian subsidiaries of overseas entities, who are actively conducting business in Australia, even if the business is otherwise predominantly conducted outside of Australia, are still mandated under the Privacy Act.

PRIVACY LAWS IN THE UNITED KINGDOM (UK)

The protection of personal data in the UK is regulated by the Data Protection Act (DPA). Like Australia's Privacy Act, it has eight principles of Data Protection which all companies collecting personal data online in the UK must follow.

1. All data shall be processed fairly and lawfully.
2. All data collected must be specific for its purpose.
3. All data collected be adequate and only for what is needed
4. All data collected must be accurate and up to date.
5. Data shall not be kept longer than needed.
6. Personal shall be processed considering people's rights.
7. All data shall be kept safe and secure. ...
8. Not be transferred outside the European Economic Area (EEA).

PRIVACY POLICY REQUIREMENTS FOR THE STANDARD FEATURES OF GOOGLE ANALYTICS

If you use Google Analytics, your privacy policy must clearly state that you use Google Analytics to track user behavior. It must also explain to the user how data their data will be collected and processed and must inform the user of the use of cookies.

PRIVACY POLICY REQUIREMENTS FOR GOOGLE ANALYTICS ADVERTISING TOOLS

If you use Google Analytics Advertising tools too, then your privacy policy requirements are even stricter. If you are doing and retargeting or remarketing, network impression reporting, interest reporting or demographic analytics you must disclose all the tools that are utilizing, and how and why you are using any of these tools. Also, you must have a notice that cookies are used by third parties and the purpose is to provide relevant advertising to the user. Finally, you must have an opt out provision and give the user instructions on how to opt out.

GOOGLE ADSENSE

If your website or mobile application (app) employs Google AdSense, there is a specific privacy policy that Google requires you to use that fully disclose that you use Google AdSense. The statement has a clear statement that third parties, including Google, use cookies for the purpose of providing specific advertising to the user based on previous browsing behavior (very stalkerish!).

You also must provide the user with information on Google's DoubleClick cookies as well as instructions on how users can opt-out of the use of DoubleClick cookies through Google's Ad Settings.

Google also mandates that you use "commercially reasonable efforts" to get user consent to use cookies on their device.

If this sounds completely foreign to you, it really is not. Think of all the pop-up banners that appear when you go to a webpage that tell you that the website uses cookies and gives you the chance to opt out and block the use of cookies.

The Cookie Monster: Additional Requirements for EU Businesses

Any country in the European Union that uses Google AdSense must do a few more things to be compliant.

EU business must further disclose the different types of cookies that are used, any details of any cookies from third parties that may be used and why cookies are used and how they are placed on devices. This can also be done with a simple pop-up banner.

COOKIES CONSENT

Consent to place cookies on a user's device requires an affirmative opt-in (just like text messages!). The user *must* affirmatively check the box before cookies can be placed on their device.

WHAT HAPPENS IF YOU DO NOT COMPLY?

The FTC (yep them again) regulates unfair or deceptive commercial practices and is the number one federal regulator of privacy rights. The FTC is the one that will bring enforcement actions against companies. A company that fails to comply with posted privacy policies and that fails to adequately protect personal information is subject to prosecution by the FTC.

There is another act called the **Children's Online Privacy Protection Act (COPPA) [1998].** This act required companies to get "verifiable parental consent" prior to collecting, using, or disclosing any personal information from minors under the age of thirteen.

This act also requires websites to post an online privacy policy, collect only the personal information necessary, and create and maintain reasonable security measures.

There is another act called the **Controlling the Assault of Non-Solicited Pornography and Marketing Act (CAN-SPAM Act) [2003]** which prohibits sending unsolicited commercial email and prohibits any misleading header information and deceptive subject lines in any commercial emails. CAN-SPAM also mandates that email senders disclose certain information and always include a valid opt-out provision in the email.

The **Financial Services Modernization Act (GLBA) [1999]** governs the way that financial institutions collect, use, and disclose personal information and requires that the institution provides customer notices. If you are an entrepreneur that has one of those lending apps then you would need to comply with this.

The **Fair and Accurate Credit Transactions Act (FACTA) [2003]** requires financial institutions and creditors to maintain written identity theft prevention programs and requires businesses to properly dispose of and destroy sensitive consumer data, security experts considered it an important step forward in the fight against consumer fraud and identity theft.

The **Electronic Communications Privacy Act (ECPA)** of 1986 is a federal statute that outlines how the government is allowed to monitor cell phone conversations and Internet communications. But beware, the astronomical advances in technology have run past the statute leaving valuable information without full protection, such as your private actions in your home through your own webcam. To fully illustrate this lack of protection and how technology ran past the ECPA, is the case of *Robbins v. Lower Merion School District* (2010), which is known as "Webcam Gate». In Webcam Gate, the plaintiff victims accused two suburban Philadelphia high schools of ECPA violations when the schools (get ready for this) remotely activated webcams embedded in school-issued laptops and spied on the students at home. The schools owned up to secretly taking over 66,000 web shots and screenshots, including webcam shots of students in their bedrooms on forty-two separate webcams!

The spyware they used was meant to track the laptops, not to spy on the students using them. In the end, the outdated ECPA had no protective law for the students; even though the school did offer a monetary settlement in the end, they were not charged criminally. Another lawmaker attempted to enact a new law in the face of the intrusion to the students, but it did not pass. The moral of the story: **COVER YOUR WEBCAM.**

Hackers beware!! The **Computer Fraud & Abuse Act (CFAA) [1986]** is a cybersecurity bill that was enacted in 1986 as an amendment to existing computer fraud law, which had been included in the Comprehensive Crime Control Act of 1984. The CFAA law prohibits people accessing a computer without authorization, or in excess of authorization. But this is not just a hacker going into a stranger's computer. The was a recent case where someone ran the license plate number for a friend, and even though he had a right to access that database, he used it for illicit purposes and therefore became a hacker!

This is just a guide to give you a heads up of what is out there. When you are hiring a marketing person or a marketing firm, ask them about their experience with compliance issues and the aforementioned acts and laws. Bring this book and use the guide to ask pointed questions to make sure you hire someone with the compliance knowledge you need.

TERMS AND CONDITIONS

Terms and conditions are a contract between you and the user that lays out the expectations of the company as well as gives information to the user.

Having a terms of service agreement on your website is not legally required (not even by the super-strict GDPR) but it would behoove you to have one as it can help liability down the road. There are also so many other benefits for both you and the user, such as maintaining control over your business platform, laying out all your rules, requirements, and restrictions. It is a great place to cover your bases (and something else!)

Also, keep in mind that even if they are not legally required, a lot of e-commerce platforms require that you have terms and conditions with certain language. Think of the Walmart Marketplace, who requires sellers to have a disclaimer regarding the sales tax imbedded in their terms and conditions.

These are some of the basic headings you will need in your terms and conditions.

- Introduction
- License
- The Right to make changes to the terms of service agreement
- Hyperlinking your content
- User guidelines (rules, restrictions, requirements)
- Copyright and intellectual property

- Governing law
- Warranty disclaimer
- Reservation of Rights
- Limitation of liability
- Disclaimers

WEBSITES WITH AFFILIATE LINKS

Also, certain rules apply to affiliate marketers. For example, affiliate marketers are required to disclose any commissions they earn from the affiliate links on the page where they display them. Affiliate marketers should add an affiliate disclaimer clause in their terms and conditions so that site visitors understand that the affiliate will be earning commissions from links on their site.

The Federal Trade Commission (FTC), who is everywhere and watching everything is the body that regulates how marketers receive commissions from brands. Other countries have similar laws and similar governing bodies, so if you are selling in the European Union, the United Kingdom, or Canada you should have that information disclosed in your terms and conditions.

Moreover, the FTC requires disclosure of any "material connection" you have to a brand whose products or services you are endorsing. The FTC takes the stance that affiliate links are a form of marketing for the products being endorsed.

The standard that the FTC uses for proper disclosures is that they must be "to be unambiguous, clear, and conspicuous." You have to be super straightforward; the disclaimer must be in the same view as the link, and don't bury any disclaimer somewhere a user won't see it.

Note, however, that certain affiliate networks, such as Amazon and Walmart, do have very specific wording that they request you to use for your disclosures as a condition to being part of their marketplace.

I suggest that you put a disclaimer such as the one below at the top of the page:

We wanted to let you know that our site contains affiliate links to products. We may receive a commission for purchases made through these links.

To place next to a specific link:
www.theentreprenuerslawgroup.com/leatherbriefcase Paid link

Site-wide disclaimer for affiliate links:
We wanted to let you know that we may receive commissions when you click our links and make purchases.

Sample Terms and Conditions
Welcome to www.TheEntrepreneursLawGroup.com!

These terms and conditions outline the rules and regulations for the use of The Entrepreneur's Law Group, LLC's website, located at www.TheEntrepreneursLawGroup.com

By accessing this website, we assume you accept these terms and conditions. Do not continue to use www. TheEntrepreneursLawGroup.com if you do not agree to take all the terms and conditions stated on this page.

The following terminology applies to the terms and conditions, privacy statement and disclaimer notice, and all agreements: "Client," "You," and "Your" refers to you, the person logged onto this website and compliant to the company's terms and conditions. "The Company," "Ourselves," "We," "Our," and "Us," refers to our company. "Party," "Parties," or "Us," refers to both the client and us. All terms refer to the offer, acceptance, and consideration of payment necessary to undertake the process of our assistance to the client in the most appropriate manner for the express purpose of meeting the client's needs in respect of provision of the company's stated services in accordance with and subject to prevailing law of Netherlands. Any use of the above terminology or other words in the singular, plural, capitalization and/or he/she or they, are taken as interchangeable, and therefore as referring to same.

COOKIES

We employ the use of cookies. By accessing www.TheEntrepreneursLawGroup.com, you agreed to use cookies in agreement with The Entrepreneur's Law Group, LLC's privacy policy.

Most interactive websites use cookies to let us retrieve the user's details for each visit. Cookies are used by our website to enable the functionality of certain areas to make it easier for people to visit our website. Some of our affiliate/advertising partners may also use cookies.

LICENSE

Unless otherwise stated, The Entrepreneur's Law Group, LLC and/or its licensors own the intellectual property rights for all material on www.TheEntrepreneursLawGroup.com. All intellectual property rights are reserved. You may access this from www.

TheEntrepreneursLawGroup.com for your own personal use subjected to restrictions set in these terms and conditions.

You must not:

Republish material from www.TheEntrepreneursLawGroup.com

Sell, rent, or sublicense material from www.TheEntrepreneursLawGroup.com

Reproduce, duplicate, or copy material from www.TheEntrepreneursLawGroup.com

Redistribute content from www.TheEntrepreneursLawGroup.com

This agreement shall begin on the date hereof.

Parts of this website offer an opportunity for users to post and exchange opinions and information in certain areas of the website. The Entrepreneur's Law Group, LLC does not filter, edit, publish, or review comments prior to their presence on the website. Comments do not reflect the views and opinions of The Entrepreneur's Law Group, LLC, its agents and/or affiliates. Comments reflect the views and opinions of the person who posts their views and opinions. To the extent permitted by applicable laws, The Entrepreneur's Law Group, LLC shall not be liable for the comments or for any liability, damages or expenses caused and/or suffered as a result of any use of and/or posting of and/or appearance of the comments on this website.

The Entrepreneur's Law Group, LLC reserves the right to monitor all comments and to remove any comments which can be considered inappropriate, offensive or causes breach of these terms and conditions.

You warrant and represent that:

You are entitled to post the comments on our website and have all necessary licenses and consents to do so.

The comments do not invade any intellectual property right, including without limitation copyright, patent, or trademark of any third party.

The comments do not contain any defamatory, libelous, offensive, indecent, or otherwise unlawful material which is an invasion of privacy.

The comments will not be used to solicit or promote business or custom or present commercial activities or unlawful activity.

You hereby grant The Entrepreneur's Law Group, LLC a non-exclusive license to use, reproduce, edit, and authorize others to use, reproduce and edit any of your comments in any and all forms, formats, or media.

HYPERLINKING TO OUR CONTENT

The following organizations may link to our website without prior written approval:

Government agencies.
Search engines.
News organizations.

Online directory distributors may link to our website in the same manner as they hyperlink to the websites of other listed businesses; and

Systemwide accredited businesses, except soliciting non-profit organizations, charity shopping malls, and charity fundraising groups, may not hyperlink to our website.

These organizations may link to our home page, to publications or to other website information so long as the link: (a) is not in any way deceptive; (b) does not falsely imply sponsorship, endorsement or approval of the linking party and its products and/or services; and (c) fits within the context of the linking party's site.

We may consider and approve other link requests from the following types of organizations: commonly known consumer and/or business information sources.dot.com community sites.

We will approve link requests from these organizations if we decide that: (a) the link would not make us look unfavorably to ourselves or to our accredited businesses; (b) the organization does not have any negative records with us; (c) the benefit to us from the visibility of the hyperlink compensates the absence of The Entrepreneur's Law Group, LLC; and (d) the link is in the context of general resource information.

These organizations may link to our home page so long as the link: (a) is not in any way deceptive; (b) does not falsely imply sponsorship, endorsement or approval of the linking party and its products or services; and (c) fits within the context of the linking party's site.

If you are one of the organizations listed in paragraph 2 above and are interested in linking to our website, you must inform us by sending an e-mail to The Entrepreneur's Law Group, LLC. Please include your name, your organization name, contact information as well as the URL of your site, a list of any URLs from which you intend to link to our website, and a list of the URLs on our site to which you would like to link. Wait 2-3 weeks for a response.

Approved organizations may hyperlink to our website as follows:

By use of our corporate name; or

By use of the uniform resource locator being linked to; or

By use of any other description of our website being linked to that makes sense within the context and format of content on the linking party's site.

No use of The Entrepreneur's Law Group, LLC's logo or other artwork will be allowed for linking absent a trademark license agreement.

IFRAMES
Without prior approval and written permission, you may not create frames around our webpages that alter in any way the visual presentation or appearance of our website.

CONTENT LIABILITY
We shall not be held responsible for any content that appears on your website. You agree to protect and defend us against all claims that are rising on your website. No link(s) should appear on any website that may be interpreted as libelous, obscene, or

criminal, or which infringes, otherwise violates, or advocates the infringement or other violation of, any third-party rights.

RESERVATION OF RIGHTS

We reserve the right to request that you remove all links or any particular link to our website. You approve to immediately remove all links to our website upon request. We also reserve the right to amend these terms and conditions and it is linking policy at any time. By continuously linking to our website, you agree to be bound to and follow these linking terms and conditions.

REMOVAL OF LINKS FROM OUR WEBSITE

If you find any link on our website that is offensive for any reason, you are free to contact and inform us at any moment. We will consider requests to remove links, but we are not obligated to or so or to respond to you directly.

We do not ensure that the information on this website is correct, we do not warrant its completeness or accuracy; nor do we promise to ensure that the website remains available or that the material on the website is kept up to date.

DISCLAIMER

To the maximum extent permitted by applicable law, we exclude all representations, warranties and conditions relating to our website and the use of this website. Nothing in this disclaimer will:

- limit or exclude our or your liability for death or personal injury.
- limit or exclude our or your liability for fraud or fraudulent misrepresentation.

- limit any of our or your liabilities in any way that is not permitted under applicable law; or
- exclude any of our or your liabilities that may not be excluded under applicable law.

The limitations and prohibitions of liability set in this section and elsewhere in this disclaimer: (a) are subject to the preceding paragraph; and (b) govern all liabilities arising under the disclaimer, including liabilities arising in contract, in tort and for breach of statutory duty.

As long as the website and the information and services on the website are provided free of charge, we will not be liable for any loss or damage of any nature. This is just an exceedingly small sample to give you an idea of what basics you should have.

Please make sure you tailor your privacy policy and terms of use to industry and your company. If you use affiliates or engage in any affiliate marketing, be sure to read the next chapter for compliance with affiliate marketing.

CHAPTER 25:

AFFILIATE MARKETING

Affiliate marketing is so popular, but it is not as simple as you may believe it to be, and a lot of influences underestimate the regulatory compliance required to stay out of hot water. Because marketing itself is very regulated, adding a third party in the mix weakens your control over content and claims. As such, affiliate marketing can be very regulated and can open a host of compliance issues and marketing problems if you do not have some tailored policies and procedure in place. That includes a solid framework of your affiliate program as well as having the proper disclaimers and disclosures.

Let us start with what affiliate marketing is, so you understand its less than obvious complexities. In basic terms, affiliate marketing is a dynamic and widely utilized form of performance-based marketing that is structured for businesses to reward individuals, known as affiliates, for driving traffic or sales to the company's products or services through the affiliate's marketing efforts.

The core concept revolves around a partnership between the merchant and the affiliate, with the latter earning a commission for each successful sale, click, or lead generated through their unique affiliate link. This model is particularly popular in the online realm, where e-commerce has flourished, enabling companies to expand their reach and increase sales without significant upfront costs.

In an affiliate marketing arrangement, affiliates typically promote products or services through various channels, such as websites, blogs, social media, or email marketing. The success of the affiliate is directly tied to their ability to effectively market and drive conversions for the merchant. Affiliates often leverage their online presence and expertise in a specific niche to attract a targeted audience that is more likely to convert. This symbiotic relationship benefits both parties: merchants gain increased exposure and sales without shouldering hefty advertising expenses upfront, while affiliates earn commissions for their promotional efforts.

One of the key advantages of affiliate marketing lies in its scalability and flexibility. Merchants can collaborate with a diverse network of affiliates, each contributing to the overall marketing strategy. This decentralized approach allows businesses to tap into various markets and audiences, adapting to changing trends and consumer behavior. Additionally, affiliates have the flexibility to choose products or services that align with their interests or cater to their audience's needs, fostering authenticity and trust within their communities. This personalized touch often results in higher conversion rates compared to traditional, less-targeted advertising methods.

The tracking and measurement of affiliate marketing performance are crucial components of this model. Advanced tracking technologies, such as cookies and affiliate tracking software, enable merchants to monitor the effectiveness of each affiliate's efforts accurately. This data-driven approach not only ensures fair compensation for affiliates but also empowers merchants to refine their marketing strategies, optimize conversions, and build lasting relationships with high-performing affiliates. Overall, affiliate marketing represents a win-win scenario, where merchants expand their market reach, and affiliates monetize their online influence by promoting products or services they genuinely believe in.

Affiliate Tracking and the Legal Issues from Gathering User Data

Tracking the affiliate's sales requires certain disclosures because they use various tools and techniques to keep track of sales analytics, monitor performance, and optimize their marketing strategies.

Affiliate Tracking Software

Affiliate marketers often rely on specialized affiliate tracking software or platforms. These tools provide unique affiliate links to marketers, allowing them to track clicks, conversions, and sales associated with their efforts.

Unique Affiliate Links

Each affiliate marketer is assigned a unique tracking link that they use in their promotional activities. This link helps attribute sales and leads back to the specific affiliate, providing accurate data on their performance.

Cookies and Tracking Pixels

Cookies are often used to track user behavior. When a user clicks on an affiliate link, a cookie is placed on their device. This cookie stores information that helps track the user's interactions, and if they make a purchase, the affiliate is credited for the sale. Similarly, tracking pixels can be used to monitor user activity on a website.

Conversion Tracking

Conversion tracking is crucial for affiliate marketers. They track not only clicks but also the actions that users take on the advertiser's site, such as making a purchase or filling out a form. This data helps affiliates understand the effectiveness of their marketing efforts.

Analytics Platforms

Many affiliate marketers integrate their tracking links with popular analytics platforms like Google Analytics. This allows them to get a more comprehensive view of user behavior, traffic sources, and other relevant data.

Dashboard and Reports

Affiliate marketers often have access to dashboards provided by affiliate programs or networks. These dashboards offer real-time data on clicks, conversions, commissions earned, and other performance metrics. They may also receive regular reports summarizing their performance.

Sub-IDs and Custom Parameters

Some affiliate tracking systems allow marketers to use sub-IDs or custom parameters. This enables affiliates to add additional information to their tracking links, helping them segment and analyze their traffic sources more effectively.

A/B Testing

A/B testing involves creating multiple versions of promotional materials to see which performs better. Affiliate marketers use A/B testing to optimize their strategies based on data-driven insights, improving their chances of driving up more sales.

Communication with Advertisers

Effective communication with advertisers is essential. Affiliate marketers may collaborate closely with the advertisers to gain insights into product performance, upcoming promotions, and any changes in the marketing strategy.

Continuous Optimization

Based on the collected data, affiliate marketers continuously optimize their campaigns. This may involve refining ad creatives, targeting specific audience segments, adjusting bidding strategies, or focusing on high-converting traffic sources.

By leveraging these tools and strategies, affiliate marketers can gain a comprehensive understanding of their sales analytics and make informed decisions to improve their overall performance so they can rake in even more revenue!

All the aforementioned methods of tracking affiliate sales come with exposure to legal problems, so maintaining transparency and complying with legal regulations is the best bet to earning a commission from sales generated through an affiliate link does require notice to the customer that the affiliate will earn a commission through a relationship with an affiliate program.

Here are common elements to include in affiliate marketing disclosures and disclaimers:

Clear and Conspicuous Disclosure

Clearly state that you may earn a commission through affiliate links.

Use language that is easy to understand and conspicuous to your audience.

Place the disclosure near the affiliate links or in a location where it is easily noticeable.

Affiliate Relationship Disclaimer

Explicitly mention your relationship with the company or product being promoted.

Example: "I may earn a small commission if you make a purchase through my affiliate link. This comes at no extra cost to you."

Affiliate Link Identification

Clearly identify affiliate links, either through a disclaimer or by using specific wording (e.g., "affiliate link," "affiliate," "commission," or similar terms).

Use of Affiliate Banners or Widgets

If you use banners or widgets containing affiliate links, disclose the affiliate relationship near or on the element itself.

Full Disclosure in Reviews and Endorsements

If you publish reviews or endorsements of products or services for which you have an affiliate relationship, disclose this information prominently.

Be honest and provide balanced information to your audience.

Disclaimer Regarding Results

If your content discusses potential results, earnings, or benefits related to a product or service, include a disclaimer that individual results may vary, and not everyone will achieve the same outcomes.

Compliance with FTC Guidelines
In the United States, the Federal Trade Commission (FTC) has guidelines for affiliate marketing disclosures. Ensure that your disclosures comply with these guidelines, which may include using clear and unambiguous language.

Consistent Disclosure Across Platforms
Maintain consistent disclosure practices across all platforms where you share affiliate links, including your website, social media channels, and emails.

Updated Disclosures
Regularly review and update your disclosures to ensure they remain accurate and comply with any changes in regulations or guidelines.

Affiliate Terms and Conditions
Implementing a clear and comprehensive policy for affiliate links on your website is crucial for several reasons. Firstly, a well-defined policy helps establish transparency and trust with your audience. By clearly outlining how and why you use affiliate links, you demonstrate a commitment to openness, which can enhance your credibility. Visitors are more likely to trust your recommendations and engage with your content when they understand the affiliate relationship.

Secondly, a robust affiliate link policy ensures compliance with legal and regulatory requirements. Many jurisdictions have specific rules governing the disclosure of affiliate relationships to protect consumers from deceptive practices. By having a policy in place that clearly communicates your use of affiliate links and how they may generate income for your site, you mitigate the risk of running afoul of these regulations. This can help you avoid legal issues and maintain a positive reputation in the eyes of both your audience and relevant authorities.

Lastly, a well-crafted affiliate link policy provides guidance to your content creators and contributors. It sets expectations regarding the appropriate use of affiliate links, ensuring consistency across your website. This consistency is essential for maintaining a professional and cohesive brand image. A policy can outline the types of products or services that align with your brand values and the acceptable practices for incorporating affiliate links into your content, helping to maintain a high standard of quality and relevance for your audience. In summary, a clear affiliate link policy is instrumental in building trust, ensuring legal compliance, and maintaining consistency across your website.

SAMPLE PRIVACY POLICY FOR AFFILIATES

Affiliate Links:
1. Disclosure:
   - We may use affiliate links on our website, which means that we earn a commission if you make a purchase using these links.
   - Our commitment is to be transparent with our audience. We will clearly disclose when a link is an affiliate link by using labels such as "Affiliate Link," "Ad," or similar identifiers.

2. Impartiality:
   - The use of affiliate links does not influence our content or recommendations. We prioritize providing accurate and unbiased information to our audience.

3. Affiliate Programs:
    - We carefully select affiliate programs and products that align with the values and interests of our audience.
    - Our participation in affiliate programs does not imply an endorsement of the products or services promoted through these links.

4. Cookie Policy:
    - Affiliate links may use cookies to track referrals. By clicking on an affiliate link, you consent to the use of cookies in accordance with our cookie policy.

5. User Responsibility:
    - Users should be aware that clicking on affiliate links may result in commissions being earned by the website. It is the user's responsibility to read and understand the terms and conditions of any product or service they purchase through affiliate links.

Privacy Policy
Introduction:

This privacy policy outlines how [Your Company Name] collects, uses, discloses, and safeguards your personal information. By using our website [Your Website URL], you agree to the terms outlined in this policy.

Information Collection:

1. Personal Information:
    - We may collect personal information such as names, email addresses, and demographic data when voluntarily submitted by our users.

2. Automatically Collected Information:
   - Our website may collect information automatically, including but not limited to IP addresses, browser types, and usage patterns. This information is used for analytical purposes and to enhance user experience.

Use of Information:

1. Communication:
   - We may use your contact information to send newsletters, updates, and promotional materials. You can opt out of these communications at any time.

2. Analytics:
   - We use collected data for analytics and to improve the functionality and content of our website.

Disclosure of Information:

1. Third-Party Services:
   - We may share your information with third-party service providers that assist in website operations, analytics, and marketing efforts. These service providers are obligated to maintain the confidentiality of your information.

2. Legal Compliance:
   - We may disclose personal information if required to do so by law or in response to lawful requests from public authorities.

Security:
We employ reasonable security measures to protect against unauthorized access, alteration, disclosure, or destruction of personal information.

Policy Updates:
This privacy policy may be updated periodically. Users will be notified of any significant changes.

Contact Information:
If you have any questions or concerns regarding this policy, please contact us at [Your Contact Email].

Date of Last Revision: [Insert Date]

[Your Company Name] [Your Company Address] [Your Company Website URL]

CHAPTER 26:

SOCIAL MEDIA INFLUENCERS

Social media has been a gamechanger in every area of life, but the area I find most fascinating is the ability to make money.

Social media influencers have now become their own business.

Think about someone selling bracelets at a farmer's market. He has a captive audience of maybe a thousand people that will walk by on one given day. Of the one thousand people, maybe 20% will be interested in buying a bracelet. Out of the 20%, maybe he will convert 10% of those people into sales. While it may be like shooting fish in a barrel to have a captive audience, he is already limited in his ability to reach more people.

He also must be physically present, set up the booth and engage people to have them look at his product.

He is already limited by the number of conversions and time.

One post on social media can reach thousands—or hundreds of thousands—of accounts while the merchant is asleep. Now the merchant decides to post interesting, funny, or informative content that aligns with his bracelet—such as connecting the bracelet to a purpose or cause. He has become one type of social media influencer. Now picture the merchant gets a few influencers to wear his bracelets, and those people have a large number of followers.

Influencers operate in various niches, including fashion, beauty, fitness, lifestyle, technology, and more. They create and share content such as posts, videos, and stories that resonate with their followers. This content can range from product reviews and tutorials to personal anecdotes and lifestyle insights. The influencer's ability to engage and connect with their audience distinguishes them as influential figures in the digital space.

In the ever-evolving landscape of digital marketing, social media influencers have emerged as powerful catalysts for brand promotion. With millions of followers, influencers possess the ability to sway consumer opinions and drive engagement. However, the rapid growth of influencer marketing has raised legal and ethical concerns, prompting governments and regulatory bodies to intervene. This article explores the intersection of social media influencers and marketing laws, shedding light on the challenges and regulations that govern this dynamic industry.

The Rise of Social Media Influencers

Social media influencers have become such integral players in the marketing ecosystem, leveraging their online presence to connect with audiences across various platforms. Influencers can be individuals, celebrities, or experts in a particular niche, and they use their authenticity and relatability to build a loyal following. Brands often collaborate with influencers to tap into their engaged audience and benefit from the trust these influencers have established.

The Influencer Marketing Landscape

Before delving into the legal aspects, it is crucial to understand the dynamics of influencer marketing. Brands engage influencers for a variety of reasons, including brand awareness, product promotion, and audience engagement. Influencers, in turn, monetize their online presence through brand partnerships, sponsored content, and affiliate marketing. The symbiotic relationship between influencers and brands has fueled the growth of an industry estimated to be worth billions of dollars. I have a client that was paid almost $1,000,000.00 to hold a vape in his hand during a podcast.

Legal Challenges in Influencer Marketing

Despite its popularity, influencer marketing faces legal challenges that require careful navigation. The following sections explore key legal considerations that influencers and brands must consider.

Disclosure and Transparency

One of the primary concerns in influencer marketing is the lack of transparency regarding sponsored content. Influencers are often required by law to disclose their relationships with brands, ensuring that their audience is aware of the promotional nature of the content. Various countries, including the United States and the United Kingdom, have specific guidelines on disclosure, and failure to comply can result in fines and reputational damage.

For instance, the Federal Trade Commission (FTC) in the U.S. mandates clear and conspicuous disclosure. Hashtags such as #ad or #sponsored are commonly used, but the placement and visibility of these disclosures must adhere to the FTC guidelines.

Truth in Advertising

In addition to disclosure, influencer content must adhere to truth in advertising standards. Making false claims about a product or service, exaggerating benefits, or endorsing products without genuine experience can lead to legal repercussions. The responsibility extends to both influencers and the brands they promote, emphasizing the importance of accurate and honest communication in marketing campaigns.

Endorsement Guidelines

In many jurisdictions, influencers are considered endorsers, and specific guidelines govern how endorsements should be conducted. These guidelines often require influencers to have personal experience with the endorsed product and ensure that their endorsements reflect honest opinions. Failure to comply with these guidelines can result in legal consequences for both influencers and brands.

Copyright and Intellectual Property

The use of copyrighted material, including images, music, and videos, in influencer content raises intellectual property concerns. Influencers must secure the necessary rights or permissions for any copyrighted material they incorporate into their posts. Brands, too, must ensure that the content they provide to influencers complies with copyright laws to avoid legal complications.

Data Privacy and Security

Influencer marketing involves the collection and sharing of data, raising concerns about privacy and security. Influencers often have access to user data, and the mishandling of this information can lead to legal repercussions. Compliance with data protection laws, such as the General Data Protection Regulation (GDPR) in the European Union, is crucial to avoid fines and maintain trust with the audience.

Regulatory Responses to Influencer Marketing
Recognizing the challenges posed by influencer marketing, regulatory bodies worldwide have implemented or proposed measures to bring greater transparency and accountability to the industry.

FTC Guidelines in the United States
The FTC in the United States has been at the forefront of regulating influencer marketing. Their guidelines emphasize the importance of clear and conspicuous disclosure, ensuring that consumers can easily identify sponsored content. The FTC has taken enforcement actions against influencers and brands that fail to comply with these guidelines, signaling a commitment to upholding truth in advertising.

Challenges in Enforcement
While regulations exist, enforcing them poses challenges in the dynamic and globalized realm of influencer marketing.

Cross-Border Transactions
Influencers often collaborate with brands and audiences across borders, making it challenging to enforce consistent regulations. Varying legal frameworks and cultural differences further complicates the task of ensuring universal compliance.

Identification of Violations
Identifying violations of marketing laws in the vast expanse of social media platforms is a significant challenge. Automated algorithms and manual reporting mechanisms are commonly

used, but the sheer volume of content makes it difficult to catch every instance of non-compliance.

Evolving Platforms and Trends
The rapid evolution of social media platforms and the emergence of contemporary trends pose challenges for regulators. As influencers explore novel ways of engaging audiences, regulators must adapt to changing landscapes to effectively address potential legal issues.

Ethical Considerations in Influencer Marketing
Beyond legal obligations, influencer marketing raises ethical considerations that influencers, brands, and regulators must address.

Authenticity and Genuine Engagement
Maintaining authenticity is essential for influencers to build trust with their audience. Faking engagement metrics, using deceptive tactics, or promoting products without genuine belief in their value can erode trust and lead to long-term damage.

Impact on Mental Health
The relentless pursuit of perfection on social media, often perpetuated by influencers, has raised concerns about its impact on mental health. Regulators and industry stakeholders are increasingly focusing on promoting responsible content creation and discouraging practices that contribute to unrealistic beauty standards and body image issues.

Child Influencers and Exploitation
The rise of child influencers has brought attention to issues of child labor laws, privacy, and exploitation. Regulators are

grappling with how to protect the rights and well-being of child influencers while ensuring that they have a normal childhood and are shielded from potential harm.

Influencer marketing offers a unique and powerful channel for brands to connect with consumers. However, the legal and ethical challenges inherent in this industry require careful consideration and adherence to regulations. As influencers, brands, and regulators navigate this complex landscape, collaboration and continuous dialogue are essential to strike a balance between fostering creativity and protecting consumers. Ultimately, a well-regulated influencer marketing ecosystem is necessary to avoid fines, lawsuits and having social media platforms shut down.

CHAPTER 27:

YOUR LEADERSHIP TEAM

In order to have a proper launch, you will need to have a corporate team in place. You may not have all these positions filled yet, and you may not need to, but having an "org chart "is like having a map or guide for direction. It is also important for attracting investors, obtaining funding, and aligning the right talent because they see the vision of where you are going.

Firstly, you as the entrepreneur should be the founder and CEO. If you are your only employee, that is okay! Just ensure you have trusted advisors for your legal and financial needs.

Your first hire should be a GREAT executive assistant who can take a lot of the time consuming tasks off your plate. If you are focused on the content and activities that grew your business and got you this far, you are operating at your highest and best use.

If you are fumbling around ordering copy paper and sending out ZOOM invites, you are NOT at your highest and best use and therefore are thwarting your own revenue stream.

Do not get caught up in the minutia or scut work.

Your next hire is at the other end of the spectrum and should be your Chief Operating Officer (COO). The CEO and the COO are parents of the company.

As a CEO and Founder, you are the entrepreneurial and enterprising disruptor looking to push limits its and create more verticals

The COO is trying to stay "in the black" and manage the analytics, metrics, and reports to forecast the health of the company.

They will clash—a lot—and that is creative progress at its best.

The COO will organize the corporation operationally, from department to department, process to process, procedure to procedure.

Launching a company involves setting up various departments to ensure smooth operations and strategic development. The specific departments needed can vary depending on the nature of the business, but here are some essential departments that are commonly found in most companies:

1. Executive Leadership:
    - CEO (Chief Executive Officer): Responsible for overall company strategy and decision-making.
    - CFO (Chief Financial Officer): Manages financial planning, budgeting, and financial reporting.
    - COO (Chief Operating Officer): Oversees day-to-day operations and ensures the company's processes are efficient.

2. Human Resources (HR):
   - HR Manager: Handles recruitment, onboarding, employee relations, and compliance.
   - Training and Development: Provides ongoing training programs for employees.
   - Payroll and Benefits: Manages employee compensation, benefits, and payroll processing.

3. Sales and Marketing:
   - Sales Team: Responsible for selling the company's products or services.
   - Marketing Team: Develops and implements marketing strategies to promote the company.
   - Customer Support: Addresses customer inquiries, concerns, and provides support.

4. Finance and Accounting:
   - Accounting Team: Manages financial transactions, bookkeeping, and financial reporting.
   - Financial Analysts: Analyze financial data and provide insights for decision-making.
   - Treasury: Manages the company's finances, including cash flow and investments.

5. Operations:
   - Supply Chain Management: Handles procurement, logistics, and inventory management.
   - Quality Control: Ensures products or services meet established quality standards.
   - Facilities Management: Oversees physical assets and office space.

6. Information Technology (IT):
   - IT Manager: Manages the company's technology infrastructure.
   - Network and Systems Administrators: Ensure the reliability and security of the company's IT systems.
   - Data Security: Implements measures to protect sensitive company and customer data.

7. Product Development/Research and Development (R&D):
   - Product Managers: Oversee the development and launch of new products or services.
   - Research and Development Team: Conducts research to innovate and improve products.

8. Legal and Compliance:
   - General Counsel or Legal Counsel: Provides legal advice and ensures compliance with laws and regulations.
   - Compliance Officers: Monitor and enforce adherence to industry regulations.

9. Public Relations (PR) and Communications:
   - PR Manager: Manages the company's public image and communication strategy.
   - Internal Communications: Ensures effective communication within the company.

10. Strategy and Business Development:
    - Strategy Analysts: Analyze market trends and competition to inform business strategy.
    - Business Development Team: Identifies and pursues new business opportunities.

These departments work collaboratively to create a well-rounded and functional organization. The size and structure of each department will depend on the company's size, industry, and specific needs. As a company grows, additional departments or specialized roles may be added to meet evolving requirements.

CHAPTER 28:

ADDING VERTICALS TO YOUR EXISTING BRAND

Pivot. That is what you do when your current product or service becomes stale or oversaturated in the market, or when your "spiel" has been overplayed and overdone. In the ever-evolving landscape of business, the key to sustained growth and resilience lies in the ability to adapt and diversify—the pivot.

Even if your core business is thriving, exploring additional verticals can not only amplify your revenue streams but also fortify your overall business strategy. There is an art and science to identifying and integrating complementary verticals to enhance and future-proof your core enterprise.

But you must be smart and tactical about this as you do not want to cannibalize your core enterprise or offer something that is so different than what you are currently doing that your current market will not be interested in. This is why before you embark on the journey of expansion, it is crucial to understand the concept of complementarity. A complementary vertical is one that synergizes with your existing business, creating a harmonious relationship that benefits both. This can range from related products or services to entirely new markets that align with your brand identity.

Do Market Research to Navigate Growth

Embarking on diversification requires a solid foundation of market research. Identify trends, consumer preferences, and emerging opportunities. Analyze your existing customer base to uncover unmet needs or desires that could be addressed through complementary verticals. A thorough understanding of the market landscape is the compass that guides your expansion strategy.

You can do this by conducting test advertisements, focus groups, surveys, free webinars to gauge interest and even just talking to your customer base to see if they find your new venture interesting.

How to Leverage Your Core Competencies

It is particularly important that you know how to truly look inward and assess your core competencies. What are your unique strengths that have propelled your core business? Now is the time for brutal self-awareness and honesty. Integrating complementary verticals that leverage these strengths can create a competitive advantage and streamline operations. For example, if your core business excels in technology, expanding into related software solutions is a great segue!

Strategic Partnerships and Collaborations

Consider forging strategic partnerships and collaborations to enter new verticals seamlessly. Collaborating with established players in the target market can provide valuable insights, reduce risks, and enhance credibility. A well-thought-out partnership can open doors to new opportunities and accelerate your entry into complementary sectors.

Maintain Your Brand Consistency

While diversifying, maintaining a consistent brand image is paramount. Consumers should easily recognize the connection between your core business and its complementary verticals. This consistency fosters trust and loyalty, making the transition into new markets more fluid.

Risk Mitigation and Diversification

Diversification inherently involves risk, but a well-calibrated approach can mitigate potential downsides. Avoid overextension by starting with smaller-scale pilot projects or phased rollouts. Monitor performance metrics closely and be prepared to pivot based on real-time data. Diversification should be a calculated expansion, not a leap into the unknown.

Adaptability and Innovation

The business landscape is dynamic, and what works today may not work tomorrow. Embrace a culture of adaptability and innovation. Encourage a mindset that is open to experimentation and learning from both successes and failures. This agility is the cornerstone of sustainable growth in a rapidly changing business environment.

Continuous Evaluation and Optimization

The journey of diversification is not a one-time event but an ongoing process. You must never stop evaluating and pivoting. Regularly evaluate the performance of your complementary verticals, gather feedback from customers, and be prepared to iterate and optimize. The ability to adapt and refine your strategy ensures long-term success and relevance in a competitive market.

The strategic integration of complementary verticals can propel your core business to new heights, offering a diversified portfolio that enhances resilience and fosters sustained growth. By understanding market dynamics, leveraging core competencies, and maintaining brand consistency, businesses can navigate the intricate path of diversification with confidence and success, and by success, I mean multiple streams of revenue!

CHAPTER 29:

WHY YOU NEED A BUSINESS COACH OR MENTOR

Having a business coach can provide numerous benefits for individuals looking to start or grow their businesses. But that is not why they are important.

My personal experience with a business coach changed how I related to people. Business coaches are experts at translating what people are saying into what they are genuinely thinking, and watching a business coach handle people in various situations is like watching a magic show—they turn objections into sales, no into yes, and nothing into something great.

The first meaningful experience I had with a business mentor was not because I had engaged him—it was because I had the luck, pleasure, and honor to work side-by side with him. I had truly little exposure to his space prior to meeting him, and I was enamored with the idea of what he provided to others. I was drawn to his energy, positivity, creative thinking, and problem solving. I began to read the books he spoke about and apply the methodologies he taught to others. I cannot leave out the fact that I developed an exceptionally large crush on him. Why?

He made me like myself. He made me want to be a better person. He inspired me. He changed how I viewed myself and I perceived the world around me. He made me grow. But that is the least of it.

He changed the chemistry in my brain to be a kinder, softer, and more refined version of myself.

He forever altered my approach to emotions and expressive behavior and taught me the art of being human. That is because business coaches have a skill set that lends itself to developing lasting relationships and deciphering the true meaning behind people's body language and words.

Business coaches are also significant role models for learning how to speak eloquently, how to make rebuttals, and how to walk away from losing situations with grace. When I lose my composure (because I am human after all) I now learn from it, own it, ponder my triggers, forgive myself, and move on.

Experience and Expertise
The right business coach has a wealth of experience and expertise in the business world. They may have faced and overcome challenges like those you are encountering, offering valuable insights and solutions that can help you avoid the mistakes that they made, therefore helping you get a revenue stream going faster. A business coach can provide guidance and direction, helping you figure out how to navigate the complexities of running a business. They can assist in setting clear goals, developing strategies, and making informed decisions. If you are new to a certain space, or only have a few years' experience, working with a business coach in that space gives you great insight into the industry as well as practical information. And maybe a contemporary.

Network and Connections

This is monumental. Building your own community takes time, and when you are busy working, it can be difficult. A business coach often has an extensive network of contacts and connections. Being mentored and coached by someone established in the industry can open doors to new opportunities, partnerships, and potential clients. Think about all the collaborations and co-ventures you can make!

Accountability

Another great benefit on the top of my list is accountability. When you are the boss, you are not held accountable to anyone but yourself. This means you never face the consequences of failing to complete your actions. Having a business coach holds you accountable to ensure you and your business are always moving forward and not spending too much time on the coach having pizza and watching reels on social media. Having a business coach provides that necessary level of accountability. Knowing that you have someone to whom to report your progress can motivate you to stay focused and committed to your goals. This is pure psychology! The psychology behind accountability is complex and involves various cognitive, social, and motivational factors, but I have whittled it down to some basic and core concepts.

Accountability can be defined as the expectation or responsibility to answer your actions and decisions. Understanding the psychological aspects of accountability can shed light on why individuals may feel a sense of responsibility, how they respond to it, and the consequences of being held accountable.

When you know you have to report your successes and failures back to a business coach, you are more likely to feel a sense of responsibility and accountability for your choices, as well as the need to please.

External rewards or consequences, such as praise, recognition, or punishment, can influence accountability. Fear of negative consequences or anticipation of positive outcomes can drive responsible behavior.

Also, accountability is reinforced through social contracts or agreements. When you commit to a task, project, or relationship, you feel a responsibility to fulfill your obligations. This speaks not only to reporting back to your business coach, by to the community you are building through their network! You will naturally want to succeed so you can receive praise; you may be thinking you do not care about praise, but that is a natural human emotion!

When you are internally motivated by a sense of purpose, passion, or personal satisfaction, you are more likely to hold yourself accountable.

Also, receiving constructive feedback and being part of a culture that supports learning from your mistakes you can enhance your accountability by acknowledging, addressing, and adjusting your shortcomings. This is crucial for personal development and growth—and when you grow so does your business.

Personal Development
Business coaching often extends beyond just business matters. A business coach can also help with personal development, enhancing your leadership skills, communication abilities, and overall mindset. When your mindset is aligned with your

purpose, and your confidence is high, you are geared up for remarkable success.

Feedback And Perspective
A business coach provides an external perspective on your business. They can offer constructive feedback, helping you see things from different angles and ensuring that you are on the right track.

Motivation And Confidence
Entrepreneurship can be challenging, and there may be times when you feel discouraged. A coach or business coach can provide motivation, encouragement, and boost your confidence during difficult periods. Talking issues out is elemental to figuring out what worked and what did not work to avoid getting stuck in a downward cycle. If you are not moving forward, they can also provide insight to your next step.

Learning from Successes and Failures
A business coach has likely experienced both success and failure in their career. Learning from their successes can inspire you, while understanding how they navigated failures can provide valuable lessons that could have been costly.

Customized Advice
A good business coach tailors their advice to your specific situation and needs. This personalized guidance can be more relevant and effective than generic advice found in books or online.

HOW TO CHOOSE THE RIGHT BUSINESS COACH
Choosing the right business coach is crucial for your professional development and the success of your business. There are lots of

moving parts to working with a coach, and you need to be careful and diligent in how you select someone. Do your research, read reviews and testimonials, and ask for references. When you have narrowed down your search, meet with them and find the one who best aligns with your needs and aspirations, and who has a communication style that works with your personality. A few factors that should take into consideration are listed below.

Experience and Expertise
Look for a coach with relevant experience in your industry or a similar one. They should understand the challenges and opportunities specific to your business.

Proven Track Record
Ask for references and case studies from previous clients. A successful track record demonstrates the coach's effectiveness and ability to bring about positive change.

Coaching Style
Consider the coaching style that resonates with you. Some coaches are more hands-on, while others take a more collaborative or directive approach. Choose a style that aligns with your preferences and learning style.

Communication Skills
A good coach should be an excellent communicator. They should be able to listen actively, ask insightful questions, and provide constructive feedback. Effective communication is crucial for a productive coaching relationship.

Goal Alignment
Ensure that the coach understands your goals and objectives. They should be able to help you set clear, achievable milestones and provide guidance on how to reach them.

Adaptability
Business environments are dynamic, and a good coach should be adaptable to changing circumstances. They should be able to adjust their approach based on your evolving needs and the changing landscape of your business.

Empathy and Emotional Intelligence
A business coach should have an elevated level of empathy and emotional intelligence. They need to understand the emotional challenges that come with running a business and provide support and guidance accordingly.

Availability and Accessibility
Consider the coach's availability and accessibility. Ensure that they can accommodate your schedule and provide ongoing support as needed.

Continuous Learning
Look for a coach who is committed to their own professional development. A coach who invests in continuous learning and stays updated on industry trends is more likely to provide valuable insights.

Clear Agreement and Contract
Before starting the coaching relationship, make sure there is a clear agreement outlining the scope of work, expectations, confidentiality, and the duration of the coaching engagement.

Having a formal contract ensures that both parties are on the same page. I am not saying this because I am an attorney, I am saying this— Well, okay, it is because I am an attorney. Business coaches can be expensive, and you do not want to make a large investment without a clear picture of what you are getting.

I suggest starting small and not making a huge investment until you are totally clear that the relationship is working. Think of it like a marriage; you do not put a ring on it the first day.

Cost and Value

While cost is a factor, focus on the value you will receive from the coaching relationship. Consider it an investment in your personal and professional growth and assess whether the potential benefits justify the cost.

Chemistry and Trust

Trust is essential in a coaching relationship; you need a coach that you respect and trust explicitly and with whom you feel comfortable sharing your challenges and goals. Chemistry and trust are vital for an effective coaching mentorship.

CHAPTER 30:

NAVIGATING GROWING PAINS

G rowth is uncomfortable. Once a business starts generating revenue, it is important to take strategic steps to ensure continued growth, stability, and long-term success. Once you start rolling in some revenue, a lot can change. You will likely be adding more team members, adding more products, gaining more customers. More money will be rolling out than rolling on, and as a result, you will have growing pains.

Growing pains cannot be avoided, but they can be navigated.

Navigating growing pains in a new company requires a strategic and adaptable approach to ensure both personal and organizational success. Firstly, fostering open communication channels is paramount. As a new and rapidly growing company, it is essential to express concerns, share insights, and seek feedback. Drop your ego and really listen to others—they have a perspective from the outside looking in and that will give you great insight into whether your approach is expanding or stunting your growth goals. You should always be conducting regular team meetings, one-on-one discussions with employees and/ or investors, and inviting constructive feedback from everyone. Constructive feedback can help identify pain points and potential solutions. Embrace a culture of transparency so you have a shared understanding of challenges and in turn can foster a collaborative environment where everyone feels heard and valued.

Secondly, adaptability is a key skill when navigating the evolving landscape of a growing company. Back to my favorite word and concept—PIVOT. You must master the art of change and be proactive in seeking opportunities for your own professional growth and development—and that of your employees. This may involve acquiring new skills, taking on additional responsibilities, or even stepping outside your comfort zone. Again, this is where a business coach is most elemental in helping you gain a mindset of flexibility and a willingness to adapt to changing circumstances as well as adding to your skill set. With the right mindset, skills, and people, you will be prepared to navigate the growing pains and position yourself for expansion.

Finally, in the growing pain stage, the dynamics within teams and across departments can shift rapidly. Investing time in developing positive working relationships can lead to a more cohesive and supportive work environment for your employees. Collaborate with other business owners and entrepreneurs, exchange knowledge, and seek support and mentorship when needed.

Employees can feel uneasy and insecure during a growth spurt when money is rolling out more than rolling in; it is crucial to never let employees feel the squeeze or hear any words of worry over accounts payable and accounts receivable matters.

Strong interpersonal connections and unreproachable leadership skills can help alleviate the stress of growing pains and create a sense of security and unity among your team members, making it easier to navigate challenges collectively without any knowledge regarding the financial status pf your company.

Here are some practical actions your business should consider:

Financial Management
Establish a robust accounting system to track income, expenses, and profits.

Create a budget and financial forecast to guide future decision-making.

Consider reinvesting profits back into the business for expansion or improvement.

Legal and Compliance
Ensure compliance with local and industry-specific regulations.

Review and update legal contracts, agreements, and business licenses as needed.

Consider consulting with legal professionals to address any potential legal issues.

Customer Satisfaction
Focus on delivering excellent customer service to build customer loyalty.

Collect and analyze customer feedback to identify areas for improvement.

Use customer satisfaction as a tool for marketing and referrals.

Marketing and Sales
Invest in marketing strategies to attract new customers and retain existing ones.

Explore new sales channels or partnerships to expand market reach.

Utilize data analytics to measure the effectiveness of marketing campaigns.

Scale Operations
Assess the scalability of current operations and adjust handle growth.

Consider hiring additional staff or outsourcing certain tasks to meet increased demand.

Evaluate and upgrade technology and infrastructure to support growth.

Innovation and Adaptation
Stay informed about industry trends and technological advancements.

Foster a culture of innovation within the company.

Be prepared to adapt to changes in the market or competitive landscape.

Risk Management:

Identify potential risks to the business and develop mitigation strategies.

Consider insurance coverage to protect against unforeseen events.

Establish a crisis management plan in case of emergencies.

Employee Development

Invest in training and development programs for employees.

Foster a positive and inclusive work environment.

Recognize and reward employee contributions to boost morale.

Diversification

Explore opportunities for product or service diversification to reduce risk.

Consider entering new markets or expanding the business into related areas.

Long-Term Planning

Develop a long-term business strategy and vision, amend your business plan and business model as needed. The key word to always have in mind is PIVOT.

Set measurable goals and regularly review progress.

Continuously assess and adjust the business plan based on changing circumstances.

Remember that each business is unique, so the specific actions taken will depend on the industry, market conditions, and the business's individual circumstances. Regularly reassessing and adapting strategies is crucial to maintaining a competitive edge and ensuring sustained success.

CHAPTER 31:

STAYING THE COURSE

Y ou are open for business, making money and life is great. What next? Well, either you are going to exit your entrepreneurial endeavor and start a new one or grow this business by adding verticals or new services. You are an entrepreneur, and you are built for adventure. Either way, you need to stay the course.

In the dynamic and somewhat wonky landscape of business, maintaining an entrepreneurial mindset is crucial for sustained success and innovation. It takes WORK, and not just work on your business, but work on yourself as well, This chapter delves into the key principles and practices that can help you foster and preserve your beautiful entrepreneurial spirit. Whether you are a seasoned entrepreneur or just aspiring to become one, the journey involves cultivating a mindset that embraces challenges, seeks opportunities, and adapts to change.

Your number one pursuit at all times is to embrace and engage in continuous learning and personal growth. This is what nurtures the restless soul of an entrepreneur because the entrepreneurial journey is in itself nothing but a continuous learning experience.

Allow yourself to fully become obsessed with growth. Stay curious, seek out new information, and remain open to diverse perspectives. Attend workshops, read voraciously, and engage with mentors to broaden your knowledge base. A commitment to ongoing learning not only keeps you ahead of industry trends but also sharpens your problem-solving abilities. It also broadens your network of peers and clientele.

Stay strong and cultivate resilience. Challenges and setbacks are inherent in any entrepreneurial venture, and quite frankly the draw for many entrepreneurs, such as me. If it were easy, it would feel basic and utterly boring to me, and I would hate it. This is because I love the disruption of certain concepts and industry standards, and because I am bulletproof, waterproof, and bombproof to adversity. I LOVE adversity because I know I will learn an amazing life skill and lesson. I developed resilience over the years, and this was essential to navigating through tough times. Embrace failures as opportunities to learn and grow. Celebrate small victories and use them as steppingstones towards your larger goals. A resilient mindset allows you to bounce back stronger after facing adversity.

Entrepreneurial endeavors are synonymous with risk. Instead of fearing uncertainty, learn to embrace it. Successful entrepreneurs assess risks carefully, make informed decisions, and view challenges as opportunities for innovation. Develop a risk-taking mindset that is calculated, strategic, and willing to step out of the comfort zone.

Entrepreneurial thinking revolves around identifying problems and creating solutions. Cultivate a habit of viewing obstacles as opportunities to innovate. Develop a proactive approach by consistently seeking ways to improve processes, products, or services. Foster a mindset that focuses on creating value for customers and solving real-world problems.

Surround yourself with like-minded individuals who share your entrepreneurial spirit. Networking provides valuable insights, support, and collaborative opportunities. Attend industry events, join entrepreneurial communities, and establish meaningful connections. A strong network not only opens doors to new possibilities but also offers a support system during challenging times.

The business landscape is constantly evolving. Entrepreneurs must be adaptable and flexible to thrive in changing environments. Develop the ability to pivot, when necessary, embrace innovative technologies, and adjust your strategies based on market dynamics. An entrepreneurial mindset requires a willingness to evolve with the ever-shifting business landscape.

A successful entrepreneur places the customer at the core of their business. Listen to customer feedback, understand their needs, and continuously refine your offerings to meet and exceed expectations. A customer-centric mindset ensures that your entrepreneurial endeavors remain relevant and responsive to market demands.

Establish clear, measurable goals for both short and long-term success. Regularly review and reassess your objectives to ensure they align with your evolving vision. Goal setting not only provides direction but also serves as a source of motivation and accountability.

Maintaining an entrepreneurial mindset is a continuous journey of self-improvement, adaptability, and innovation. By embracing a culture of learning, resilience, and customer-centricity, entrepreneurs can navigate the complexities of the business world and consistently drive success. The principles outlined in this chapter serve as a guide for cultivating and preserving the entrepreneurial spirit in an ever-changing landscape.

CHAPTER 32:

THE EXIT AND THE ART OF LETTING GO

Selling a business is like orchestrating a symphony. It requires meticulous planning, a strategic mindset, and a harmonious blend of financial acumen and emotional intelligence.

PREPARING FOR THE SALE

Before you even contemplate selling, take a critical look at your business. Is it operating at its peak efficiency? Are there areas for improvement? It is essential to ensure that your financials are in order, your operations are streamlined, and your team is functioning cohesively. Potential buyers will scrutinize every aspect of your business, so presenting a well-oiled machine will enhance its appeal.

Engage professional advisors—financial analysts, legal experts, and business brokers—early in the process. Their insights will be invaluable as you prepare for the sale, helping you understand your business's true value and addressing any potential red flags.

VALUATION: KNOWING YOUR WORTH

First, put your ego aside, Forget how much you loved building this business. There is knowing your worth and there is knowing your value—these are two differing concepts.

Determining the value of your business is both an art and a science. While financial metrics play a crucial role, factors such as brand value, customer base, and growth potential are equally important. Collaborate with your financial advisors to conduct a comprehensive valuation, considering both tangible and intangible assets. A realistic understanding of your business's worth is crucial for setting a competitive yet attractive asking price.

Your business is not just a set of financials; it is a story. Craft a compelling narrative that encapsulates the essence of your business—its journey, achievements, and future potential. Develop a detailed information memorandum that serves as a guide for potential buyers, giving them insight into what makes your business unique and why it is a lucrative investment.

Diversify your outreach to attract a pool of potential buyers. Utilize online platforms, industry networks, and business brokers to cast a wide net. This approach not only increases your chances of finding the right buyer but also creates competition, which can drive up the sale price.

Confidentiality is key during this phase. Ensure that only serious and qualified buyers have access to sensitive information about your business. Non-disclosure agreements can provide an additional layer of protection. While and NDA cannot stop people from talking, it can give you legal recourse and compensate you for any damages from the breach of confidentiality.

NEGOTIATIONS

Negotiation is an art form that requires finesse. Be prepared to negotiate not only the sale price but also the terms and conditions of the deal. Consider the buyer's motivations and seek common ground that aligns with the interests of both parties.

Maintain transparency but be strategic in what you disclose. A balance between openness and protecting sensitive information is crucial for a successful negotiation. Your team of advisors will play a pivotal role in guiding you through this intricate dance.

Due Diligence: The Devil in the Details (like for REAL)

Once an offer is on the table, the buyer will conduct due diligence to validate the information you have provided. Be prepared for a thorough examination of your financials, contracts, operations, and legal matters. Anticipate questions and ensure that your records are meticulously organized. This phase can be time-consuming, so patience and cooperation are paramount.

THE LEGAL FINALE: SEALING THE DEAL

As negotiations solidify and due diligence concludes, legal documentation takes center stage. Work closely with your legal team to draft and review contracts, ensuring that the terms align with your expectations and protect your interests. The final agreement should address not only the purchase price but also any ongoing involvement you may have in the business, transition plans, and potential contingencies.

WHAT'S NEXT?

With the ink dry on the deal, a mix of emotions will wash over you. It is the end of one chapter but the beginning of another. Take the time to celebrate your achievements, acknowledge the impact on your team, and prepare for the next phase of your life. Your business has been your focus for so long, and the absence of that is akin to losing a friend. Allow yourself time to mourn the loss (so to speak) and do not use avoidance behavior to fill the void. Truly take the time to decide what your life will look like moving forward after having a few empty days to get your head straight about what you want to do next.

Selling a business is a transformative process that demands resilience, foresight, and a strategic mindset. As you navigate these steps, remember that each decision should align with your long-term goals. The symphony of selling a business is complex, but with the right preparation and guidance, it can be a harmonious transition to the next stage of your entrepreneurial journey.

THE START-UP CHECK LIST

TASK OR ACTION	DATE COMPLETED
1. Evaluate business idea	
2. Determine if business type requires permits, insurance, or license, apply for them if needed	
3. Create profile of target customer	
4. Write action plan	
5. Write business plan	
6. Create business model	
7. Draft mission statement	
8. Choose legal entity and incorporate	
9. Draft and execute Operating Agreement or Corporate Bylaws	
10. Get an EIN from the IRS	
11. Open a business bank account	
12. Set up Accounting department, choose software, choose accounting basis	
13. Create Merchant Accounts to accept payments via credit card	
14. Apply for startup capital	
15. Set up Marketing Department, draft marketing plan	
16. Set up IT Department	
17. Create website and social media accounts	
18. Register domain name, apply for Trademarks	
19. Set up Sales Department	
20. Set up CRM	
21. Set up office space; check insurance requirements	
22. Set up Human Resource Department	
23. Draft Employee Handbook and the Corporate Policy and Procedure Manual	
24. Draft Employee onboarding and termination documents	
25. Create sales process plan	
26. Create marketing compliance process	
27. Create and implement marketing plan	
28. Hire Employees	

29. Train employees	
30. Evaluate what is working; pivot if needed	
31. Schedule promotions; collaborate with influencers	
32. Update your Org Chart	
33. Check your mindset; hire a business coach or mentor	
34. Start selling!	

ABOUT THE AUTHOR

Courtney Jared Bannan is a distinguished attorney, law professor, author, speaker, and entrepreneur, renowned for her multifaceted expertise and visionary leadership in the legal field. Armed with a Juris Doctor degree with a concentration in International and Comparative Law and a Bachelor of Science in Business and Finance, Ms. Bannan has seamlessly merged legal acumen with business insight throughout her career.

Recognizing the profound impact of mindfulness on overall well-being, Ms. Bannan embarked on a transformative journey to India to become a certified Vinyasa yoga teacher. Ms. Bannan believes she can reshape the legal profession by integrating mindfulness into legal practice.

Legal Education and Admissions: Ms. Bannan's academic journey began in Business and Finance, which reflects her commitment to assisting the corporate sector. Her Juris Doctor degree, with a specialized focus on International and Comparative Law, has equipped her with a global perspective crucial in navigating the complexities of international legal landscapes. Ms. Bannan was a founding editor of the International Law Journal and published many articles and white papers on International Business and Caribbean Law. Admitted to practice law in Florida, New York, and Texas, Ms. Bannan also holds the esteemed designation of Certified In-House Counsel in Arizona. Her proficiency extends to the federal level, where she is barred in the United States District

Courts for the Northern, Middle, and Southern Districts of Florida, as well as the United States District Court of Appeals for the 11th Judicial Circuit.

Academic Leadership: As a law professor, Ms. Bannan imparts her wealth of knowledge and practical insights to aspiring attorneys, specifically guiding them on the entrepreneurial path. Her commitment to fostering a new generation of legal entrepreneurs underscores her dedication to shaping the future of the legal profession.

Entrepreneurial Ventures: Ms. Bannan is the driving force behind The Entrepreneur's Law Group, a boutique law firm meticulously tailored to meet the unique needs of entrepreneurs, start-ups, and large enterprises with expanding verticals. Her leadership has positioned the firm as a trusted ally for those navigating the intricacies of the business world. Additionally, Ms. Bannan is the Founder of a tech start up and creator of a revolutionary legal app "dSkribe" that will disrupt the legal industry.

Legal Expertise: With over two decades of legal experience, Ms. Bannan's proficiency spans an impressive array of practice areas, including Multifamily Commercial Real Estate, Commercial Real Estate Transactions, Residential Real Estate, Corporate Law, International Law, Intellectual Property, Mergers and Acquisitions, Securities, Crowdfunding, Media and Entertainment law, Business Litigation, Franchising and Licensing Law, Technology Law, Advertising and Social Media Law, and Data and Privacy Law. Her comprehensive skill set is a testament to her adaptability and mastery across diverse legal domains.

Career Trajectory: Ms. Bannan's journey began as a litigator, where she cultivated her legal skills in the courtroom. Progressing through the ranks, she eventually assumed the role of Chief Legal Officer in several major corporations, including a leading FinTech entity. This trajectory allowed her to amass a wealth of experience across multiple facets of the law.

Literary and Entrepreneurial Pursuits: Before embarking on her legal career, Ms. Bannan distinguished herself as a writer and editor for various publications, showcasing her prowess in communication and analysis. Her forthcoming book, *"Ready, Set, Launch,"* slated for publication in 2024, is poised to be a valuable resource for entrepreneurs navigating the legal landscape.

Ms. Bannan's innovative spirit and commitment to pushing the boundaries of traditional legal practice underscore her as a trailblazer in the intersection of law, finance, and technology. Courtney Jared Bannan stands as an exemplary figure, seamlessly integrating academia, entrepreneurship, and legal practice, leaving an indelible mark on the legal profession.

www.courtneyjaredbannan.com

https://www.instagram.com/courtneyjaredbannanesquire/

9 798990 279810